IMPLEMENTING
*A Lean
Management
System*

IMPLEMENTING
A Lean
Management
System

THOMAS L. JACKSON
with Karen R. Jones

Publisher's Message by Norman Bodek

PRODUCTIVITY PRESS
Portland, Oregon

Productivity, Inc.
P.O. Box 13390
Portland, OR 97213-0390
United States of America
Telephone: (503) 235-0600
Telefax: (503) 235-0909
E-mail: service@productivityinc.com

Cover design by William Stanton
Cover photograph by Bob Waldman
Page design by Shannon Holt
Page composition and graphics by Rohani Design, Edmonds, Washington
Printed and bound by Edwards Brothers in the United States of America

Library of Congress Cataloging-in-Publication Data

Jackson, Thomas Lindsay, 1949–
    Implementing a lean management system / Thomas L. Jackson with Karen R. Jones
        p.   cm.
    Includes index.
    ISBN: 1-56327-085-4 (hc)
    1. Industrial management.   2. Quality function deployment.   3. Strategic planning.   I. Jones, Karen R., 1954–   II. Title.
    HD31.J233   1995
    658.4—dc20   95-35473
                                                                      CIP

05 04   10 9 8 7

for Daksha

Contents

Publisher's Message

THE LEAN MANAGEMENT SYSTEM is a complete program that aligns and integrates long-term strategic development planning and day-to-day improvement targets to make your company customer-focused, flexible, and ready for tomorrow's challenges. Too often, manufacturing companies experience a huge gulf between top management's vision for the future and the day-to-day activities of everyone else in the firm. Company leaders may be inspired and knowledgeable, but often they lack the means to inspire or empower people to respond effectively to customer needs and competitive threats. *Implementing a Lean Management System* shows you how to support your company's transformation by linking strategic management to companywide activities that further the corporate vision.

What does it mean to be a lean company? Lean management is about operating the most efficient and effective organization possible, with the least cost and *zero* waste. It is an approach that requires companies to make smart use of their resources—their technology, their equipment, and above all, the knowledge and skills of their people. Lean management is about running a competent company; management must be aware of the company's capabilities and ensure that they are used appropriately.

Lean means no fat—no waste. Lean management adopts the zero-waste principles of the famous Toyota production system—the world pioneer in lean management—but goes further to address the waste inherent in bureaucratic communication and reporting systems. Think about the path information follows in most companies to get from the customer to the teams or individuals who can act on it. In most companies, communication through layers of management and across functional areas can be like the children's game called "Telephone": A message that starts out clear is repeated from person to person, and when it eventually gets to the last party it is completely garbled. In companies, it's hard to communicate through the fat of bureaucracy. Many of the successful lean companies have relatively flat organizational pyramids to begin with; others find ways to use cross-functional management to ensure that critical information is not buried or twisted before it can be used. In *Implementing a Lean Management System*, Tom Jackson offers a practical methodology for this, based on continuous improvement methods, cross-functional management, and employee involvement. The entire system is supported by documents and forms that guide the reader in applying the concepts.

Developed by senior members of Productivity, Inc., the Lean Management System provides simple guidelines and tools company leaders need to

- diagnose the company's condition in nine key areas of manufacturing excellence linked to zero waste
- develop a companywide vision, analyze strategic capabilities needed in the future, and create a five-year plan for developing those capabilities
- transform the development plan into an annual improvement policy and deploy it throughout the organization
- monitor and guide companywide activities to ensure progress toward the annual policy targets, using a cross-functional system of reporting and analysis

Implementing a Lean Management System is designed to lead company management systematically through these activities to form an unbeatable, world class operation. "World class" is a dynamic state that requires constant refinement to a level that goes beyond yesterday's best. To keep their companies best in the world, top management has to maintain a long-range vision and plan for development, but that's not enough. Everything changes. Corporate leaders in the best companies never rest on past success. Leaders of lean companies recognize that the market will change in unpredictable ways, and they shape and position their organization for flexible response to new customer demands. Even when the company has achieved a high level at lean production, they envision even higher goals to sustain their success. They learn relentlessly, bringing in the latest methodology for delivering quality, cost, development and production time, and other outputs that matter to customers. The Lean Management System inspires company leaders to this dynamic mindset through a concept Jackson calls Delta Zero—a moving target that keeps the organization working toward zero waste in all its aspects. Implementing a Lean Management System introduces model documents and forms that will help you stay on track as you continually redefine the company goals and the actions that will move you closer to them.

The Lean Management System is intended to help managers fundamentally reorganize the flow of information throughout the company so that all employees, from the front line to the boardroom, understand the company's goals and their own roles in achieving the goals. Success at large-scale projects requires communication support that spreads knowledge quickly. It would be unimaginable to attempt a military campaign without reliable communication to orchestrate the movements of troops, aircraft, and ships, telling them exactly where to be, what to do, and when to do it. Likewise, constructing an office building on schedule requires clear plans and deadlines for every essential step, from the foundation to the framing, plumbing, electrical, heating and cooling, roofing, landscaping, and so on. Building a lean organization requires similar attention to details of everyday work to reach the company's improvement targets. The Lean Management System makes this simple with monthly and daily planning forms that keep every employee aware of not only individual and team targets but specific target-related activities they will pursue in that period. The planning forms are complemented by easy-to-use reporting forms that tell managers and cross-functional teams about progress and problems to address.

The forms and examples in the book will serve as a model framework for supporting lean management in any company. We have deliberately designed the system so that managers can customize it and adapt it to fit their company's specific requirements.

Part I of the book introduces basic concepts and definitions in the Lean Management System. It describes the past and future of lean management and tells why every manufacturer should understand what it takes to succeed at it. The elements and stages of the Lean Management System are summarized here, then treated in depth in Parts II and III.

Part II deals with the Business Renewal Cycle, a long-term planning activity in which company leaders set the direction for the next three to five years. This process begins with developing a vision for the whole organization—a carefully crafted statement of the company's dynamic hopes for the future. The process of vision building involves the entire company as well as outside stakeholders to ensure that it will be a shared vision that speaks for all.

With the vision as a guide, the top management team researches the company's competitive position using traditional strategic planning information like market share analysis. Then the managers apply their knowledge about customers and competitors to diagnosis the company's strengths and weaknesses in applying lean management to attain the vision. As an aid in this, we share an assessment model—Corporate Diagnosis—based on the nine key elements of lean management we have observed in our experience with the world's best companies. (The process and application of this audit are described in detail in a companion volume, *Corporate Diagnosis: Meeting Global Standards for Excellence*). The result of the diagnosis is a snapshot of the company's capabilities. Based on this picture, the management team creates a development plan that sets improvement goals for the next three to five years, goals that will be pursued systematically through several rounds of the Strategic Improvement Cycle.

Part III of the book is about the Strategic Improvement Cycle, a four-phase event in which the development plan is deployed throughout the organization through increasingly concrete targets and specific activities during daily work. This easy-to-understand form of hoshin planning provides a framework for assuring that everyone's day-to-day improvement activities are tied to real company goals—and that the results quickly feed back to the planners who set the targets. This is where the daily and monthly planner forms and reports are used to quickly share information throughout the company. This cycle offers a vehicle for more effective cross-functional communication—essential in speeding up a company's learning and response to change. Each Strategic Improvement Cycle wraps up with a Corporate Diagnosis to check the company's progress toward its vision and development plan. The management team then adjusts the targets as needed for the next cycle of improvement activities.

This book is intended to give you, the company leader, what you need to turn your own organization into a Lean Management System. Don't expect it to happen overnight. Too many companies carry a "Flavor-of-the-Month" attitude about their change initiatives. This reminds us of an overweight person who tries a popular crash diet, becomes slim, looks in the mirror and thinks "This is terrific," then forgets about the diet. You know the result—the fat comes back. We urge you to take a long-term view of what it will take to produce and sustain real change in your company. Lean management's integration of strategic planning and daily action through companywide communication is a subtle but powerful approach that will take several cycles to get firmly rooted. The increased effectiveness you will witness is worth the wait.

Productivity, Inc. has been teaching the elements of lean management and lean production since the late 1970s when the company first led study missions to Toyota and other Japanese industrial leaders, and brought to the West the ideas of Shigeo Shingo, developer of the Toyota production system. Since that time our consultants, trainers, and publications have helped thousands of companies in the United States and around the world learn how to implement lean methods, and we have learned in turn from their experiences. This book represents the distillation of many years of experience with the world's best strategies for manufacturing, and we are pleased to share it with you.

We express our appreciation to Tom Jackson for bringing his wisdom and experience to this practical approach to strategic integration and to Karen Jones for content collaboration and feedback in organizing and clarifying the text and illustrations. Thanks also to Diane Asay, editor in chief for Productivity Press, who saw the value in a published expression of this learning and encouraged its development. Vivina Ree provided essential editorial work on the manuscript in its early stages. Connie Dyer, director of TPM research and development for Productivity, Inc., contributed substantially to the definition of lean management key areas and control points, and to the Progress Tables used in *Corporate Diagnosis.* Productivity Press art director Bill Stanton created the cover design. The pages were designed by Shannon Holt, and art and type were composed by Rohani Design. Susan Swanson managed the prepress, with editorial assistance from Julie Zinkus and Aurelia Navarro. Catchword, Inc. created the index.

Norman Bodek
Publisher

Acknowledgments

FOR THE INSPIRATION TO WRITE this book, I thank Norman Bodek, the founder and CEO of Productivity, Inc. For many years, Mr. Bodek has wished for a relatively simple, integrated approach to implementing the lean production revolution that he discovered in Japan in the late 1970s. I also thank Mohan Marendran, managing director of QDOS Microcircuits in Kulim, Malaysia, who expressed the same wish when I began consulting with QDOS in 1994. In writing this book, I have tried to create a clear and concise method for the initial implementation and sustained development of lean production systems.

Sincere thanks to Kevin Hooper, managing director of Nissan Casting Australia, and to Graeme Luxford and all the Nissan Casting personnel. In 1994 and 1995, I had the opportunity to consult with the Nissan Casting management team to conduct shopfloor training in preparation for Nissan's implementation of hoshin management and total productive maintenance. The case example in this book and the companion volume, *Corporate Diagnosis,* was developed out of that unique and enjoyable experience. Thanks also to Mssrs. Marshall Sutherland and Iain McGregor of Productivity Australia, who made that experience possible.

For intellectual input, I must acknowledge the late Taiichi Ohno and Shigeo Shingo, who first created lean production at the Toyota Motor Company. I must also mention a little-known but critical contribution of quality guru Kaoru Ishikawa to Ohno's and Shingo's production system. Ishikawa, most famous for his fishbone diagram, implemented hoshin management at Toyota in the early 1960s, and in the process created cross-functional management. With the exception of Yasuhiro Monden, writers on the subject of the Toyota production system invariably emphasize just-in-time, quick changeover, inventory reduction, and other highlights of Ohno's and Shingo's engineering innovations. But both hoshin management and cross-functional management have been an integral part of the Toyota production system since 1962, when Toyota first won the Deming Prize. The work of Ohno, Shingo, and Ishikawa embodied in the Toyota production system—including its system of management—is the real foundation of this book.

I must also thank several interpreters of the Toyota system, including Japan Management Association consultant Kenichi Nakamura, Deming Prize winner Ryuji Fukuda, and Hoshin expert Yoji Akao, as well as Alberto Galgano for his lucid explanation of Hoshin. For recognizing the value of my work and pushing me to publish this material, and for keeping me focused on the essentials of the lean management method I am indebted to Diane Asay, editor in chief of Productivity Press. For indispensable assistance in explaining the intricacies of Fukuda's CEDAC process, the X-Type Matrix, and the process of catchball, I thank Productivity consultant Tom Fabrizio. Special thanks go to Productivity consultant Constance Dyer, one of the world's leading experts in the field of lean production, who reshaped the system Keys and control points on which the Lean Management System is based, and totally rewrote the extensive Progress Tables that form the core of the companion volume, *Corporate Diagnosis*. Finally, my tremendous gratitude goes to Karen Jones, senior editor for the project, who rewrote and reorganized many sections of the book, and added the explanatory details for many of the steps of the process, all the while insuring that clarity prevails over the depth of detail we have included.

For the opportunity to start a consulting practice in Southeast Asia, I thank my in-laws, Mr. and Mrs. J.N. Patel and family, and especially their sons Hemant and Dinesh. The rich experience I gained through this business venture transformed me from a university professor into a manufacturing consultant. Finally, I thank my wife Daksha, sister-in-law Kalyani, and nieces Sunaina and Miheka, who tolerated my compulsive behavior when I was stricken daily by my technically inclined Muse.

Tom Jackson

PART I

*An Introduction to
the Lean Management
System*

Failure of existing rules is the prelude to a search for new ones.

—Thomas Kuhn

CHAPTER 1

What Is Lean Management?

THE LEAN PRODUCTION REVOLUTION IS HERE. On the shop floor, lean production applies the logic of continuous improvement, deploying cross-functional teams, small groups, and individual employees to discover, analyze, and eliminate waste in production processes. This revolution promises great benefits: dramatically reduced manufacturing and product lead times, higher labor efficiency and quality, greater market flexibility, longer machine life, lower inventories, and an end to skyrocketing overhead. Womack, Jones, and Roos from MIT predict that lean production will become the standard production system of the twenty-first century.[1] No industry, whether in manufacturing or services, will be the same again.

But there is still a long way to go. Many business leaders still think of the future in terms of growth, and they think of growth like Texans—the bigger the better. Not enough business leaders stop to ask *why* they are in business. Rather than managing change, they react to it. Equating growth with size, these companies implement "strategic planning" by multiplying the previous year's sales volumes and profits by a growth factor derived from the value of the company's stock. More sophisticated planning is reserved for the acquisition of new markets and new businesses. Sustaining growth in terms of physical expansion and short-term profit results, wherever it is headed, defines the old way of thinking.

While being big certainly has its advantages, it is more effective today to be fast, innovative, and flexible. Consequently, there is a need to redefine organizational growth or success. Successful organizations are coming to be described as those with the ability to adapt creatively to challenges. In such enlightened companies, growth is characterized more by organizational evolution than by simple multiplication. The success of lean companies such as Toyota, Hewlett-Packard, and Motorola is founded on their ability to renew themselves again and again as they skillfully face the changes that inevitably come their way.

Lean production is revolutionary because it upsets the normal relationships between price, quantity, quality, and profit. Traditional managers believe that the means for gaining profit can be expressed in the formula

$$\Pi = Q \bullet (P - C)$$

where Π = profit,
                 Q = quantity sold,
                 P = price per unit, and
                 C = cost per unit.

The formula assumes that the quantity of products sold and the price and cost to produce them are the three areas where management may control, or at least attempt to control, profit. The major profit strategy in mass production was based on economies of scale, a principle that allowed companies to lower costs as they increased the production quantity. In the grossest terms, mass production meant cheap, standardized imitations of craft production items. Economies of scale enabled mass producers to charge low prices because the more they produced, the cheaper goods became. But as anyone might tell you, a Model T is not a Rolls Royce.

THE POWER OF LEAN PRODUCTION

With the advent of lean production, the rules have changed. According to the logic of mass production, the better the quality the higher the price. Lean production systems produce high quality goods at costs that are not proportionately high. Taiichi Ohno and Shigeo Shingo, cocreators of the Toyota production system, first implemented the waste-eliminating methods which demonstrated that high quality does not necessarily demand high cost. The huge success of the Toyota company and of many other companies that adopted Toyota methods bears testament to their principles. The Toyota production method was in fact the precursor to lean production.

A lean production system can reduce overall costs—especially indirect costs—while maintaining quality standards *and* reducing manufacturing cycle time. A lean company can make twice as much product of twice the quality in half the time and space, at half the cost—with a fraction of the normal work-in-process inventory.

So powerful is lean production that even low-wage producers in developing countries find it difficult to compete because their quality is often not up to the new standard. The competitive advantages enjoyed by mass producers—even technically proficient mass producers—have been undermined completely. In rich and poor countries alike, mastering lean production is the only option for companies that hope to be players in the next millennium.

What is it about lean production that differentiates it from mass production? Lean production forges the technological mastery of mass production with the preindustrial respect for the individual's autonomy as a craftsperson. The major differences between mass production and lean production are outlined in Figure 1-1.

Although the advantages of changing to lean production clearly outweigh arguments for maintaining traditional methods of mass production, only a few companies (the winners in the pack) have converted to this proven method for maximizing resources.

Lean Production Requires Lean Management

The majority of companies still clinging to mass production methods do so for several reasons. First, the setup of a lean production system requires assistance and time. A company that is not thinking in the direction of long-term growth will not have the patience to persevere until the new system is firmly in place. Second, the process of transforming a company from mass to lean requires many physical procedural changes, often accompanied by major upheavals in company structure and processes. A company that doesn't have the courage, or doesn't (yet) hear the wolf at the door will not feel a great compulsion to turn itself inside out and stick through the

	MASS	LEAN
CUSTOMER SATISFACTION	Make what engineers want in large quantities at statistically acceptable quality levels; dispose of unused inventory at fire-sale prices.	Make what customers want with zero defects, when they want it, and only in the quantities they order.
LEADERSHIP	Leadership by executive fiat and coercion.	Leadership by vision and broad participation.
ORGANIZATION	Individualism and military-style bureaucracy.	Team-based operations and flat hierarchies.
EXTERNAL RELATIONS	Based on price.	Based on long-term relations.
INFORMATION MANAGEMENT	Information-poor management based on abstract reports generated by and for managers.	Information-rich management based on visual control systems maintained by all employees.
CULTURE	Culture of loyalty and obedience; subculture of alienation and labor strife.	Harmonious culture of involvement based on long-term development of human resources.
PRODUCTION	Large-scale machines, functional layout, minimal skills, long production runs, massive inventories.	Human-scale machines, cell-type layout, multiskilling, one-piece flow, zero inventories.
MAINTENANCE	Maintenance by maintenance specialists.	Equipment management by production, maintenance and engineering.
ENGINEERING	Model of the isolated genius, with little input from customers and little respect for production realities.	Team-based model, with high input from customers and concurrent development of product and production process design.

FIGURE 1-1.
MASS PRODUCTION VS. LEAN PRODUCTION

uncomfortable chaos known as change. Third, the metamorphosis into leanness undergone by a mass production company must be desired, decided upon, and—most important—driven by its leader. If the CEO, president, or owners are unaware of or uncommitted to lean *management,* lean production is not likely to happen.

The old style of leadership was and is autocratic, in keeping with the vertical bureaucratic organizations of the mass production era. In mass production systems, customers buy what's available, suppliers are disciplined through intense price competition, and workers do what they're told. Machines seem to matter more than human beings.

Mass production managers are not required to mingle with hourly shopfloor workers; only the rare ones do. As the mass production ethos does not embody a clear-cut policy for leaders to be informed by workers, only the most enlightened mass production leaders visit the shop floor for first-hand observation. And since this kind of "hands-on" leadership is up to the management style of the individual manager, most mass production organizations do not expect their managers to participate as team members alongside workers further down their steeply constructed hierarchies. Such inattention by managers and management systems generally invites horizontal—and vertical—bands of isolation. And competition among and within these bands consumes valuable corporate resources.

Lean management, by contrast, invites vertical, horizontal, and diagonal bands of cross-functional coordination and cooperation—and never isolation. Lean management helps a company realign its pathways of authority so that leaders and managers are expected to contribute their skills within the context of teams. It aligns company functions to compete not against each other but against the firm's competitors, and also against its most difficult adversary—organizational inertia. Any latent autocratic tendencies among managers are replaced with team-work, team-play, and team-building.

The new style of leadership is driven by the need for quality, speed, and flexibility, requiring constant and clear communication in many directions: between the company and its customers, between the company and its suppliers, and between the company and all its employees. In a lean workplace, people matter more, and maintaining the proper relation between people and machines becomes one of leadership's key objectives. Neither lean leadership nor effective lean communication paths can emerge overnight.

The Lean Management System

A mass company cannot become a lean one overnight; a rushed and superficial management effort will not yield the result. To support lean production, management must build, nurture, and support the logic and machinery that drives lean production. Lean management is actually a sophisticated practice built around several key conceptual and physical tools. It is about looking at your company in an entirely different way, describing its processes with a new vocabulary.

The process that delivers lean management has been designed, tested, and refined into what we call the Lean Management System. This system reflects the principles and methodologies of leading international managers and consultants, including Shigeo Shingo, Taiichi Ohno, Yoji Akao, Ryuji Fukuda, Shigehiro Nakamura, Hiroyuki Hirano, and Shoji Shiba. Additionally, the Lean Management System draws the best from the structures and criteria of the world's leading awards for manufacturing and quality. Developed by experienced members of Productivity, Inc. and incorporating years of intense study and focused practice among leading companies, the Lean Management System is a comprehensive approach that builds, promotes, and sustains lean production.

This book introduces the Lean Management System. Although managers at any level can benefit from this book, it is primarily addressed to the individuals who can best effect lean management throughout the company—the president or CEO and his or her direct reports. It is this top management team that will pave the path that transforms a mass system into a lean one.

HOW LEAN MANAGEMENT IMPROVES STRATEGIC PLANNING

Despite the innovative qualities of lean management, it does share some features with traditional strategic planning. In fact, the practice of lean management encompasses most of what traditional strategic planning experts say a company should do. Like traditional companies wanting to improve, lean companies analyze their own strengths and weaknesses against those of their suppliers and competitors. They study their customers and their needs, continuously scanning their environments for opportunities and threats. They identify gaps between what can be done and what must be done to stay competitive. They understand their distinctive competencies and the key factors that determine success in their markets. In addition, however, lean management overcomes the weaknesses of traditional strategic planning by incorporating four innovations:

- a "policy bridge" between top management's development plan and day-to-day implementation of learning and improvement

- a framework for continuous organizational learning and development
- employee involvement through team activities
- cross-functional management

A "Policy Bridge" to Implementation

First, lean management provides the link so often missing between top management's long-range strategic plan and the daily activities of the rest of the organization that are expected to bring about the planned results. In the Lean Management System, top management's Business Renewal Process creates a development plan with achievement milestones for the next three to five years. Then, through a series of strategic improvement cycles, management turns these long-range goals into more specific annual objectives and a policy for working toward these objectives in every part of the organization. Through interactive teamwork on all levels, the policy is deployed, adjusted, and adopted. Learning and improvement take place companywide based on this policy, and the theme of the policy is revised in each annual strategic improvement cycle.

The Lean Management System uses an adaptation of hoshin management (also called policy deployment), an approach developed in highly successful Japanese manufacturing organizations for aligning the entire workforce with top management's vision and goals. In a full implementation of hoshin management, the system is used to drive daily production as well as breakthrough improvement efforts. In this book we will focus on applying the system to a few critical breakthrough improvement areas each year. After a company learns the process through several improvement cycles and gets closer to excellence in lean management, top management can use the same policy deployment approach to support continuous improvement in all areas.

Organizational Learning

Second, lean management views the entire company not only as a vehicle for action, but as a dynamic learning entity that grows by acquiring new organizational capabilities. This approach requires a company to establish baselines for improvement by diagnosing itself in nine key areas of lean management (introduced on page 14 and described in Chapter 2) and benchmarking against its competitors. To stay ahead of the industry learning curve, lean management consciously provokes learning by periodically establishing challenging new targets for each key factor.

Employee Involvement

Third, lean management extends the involvement of employees from shop floor to strategic planning. Through employee involvement at the shopfloor level, top managers learn in detail about their operating conditions and acquire creative insights for improvement. Employee involvement in strategic planning works in much the same way, by helping top managers gather detailed information about the company's overall strategic condition from the frontline sources. Likewise, it permits a company to capture innovative ideas from individuals throughout the organization, ideas that may be developed into strategic advantages in the future.

Cross-Functional Management

Fourth, lean management is specifically designed to operate in a flat, cross-functional, team-based organization, as illustrated in Figure 1-2. Mass production organizations govern themselves by means of management ladders patterned after the military-style hierarchies created by DuPont and General Motors in the late nineteenth and early twentieth centuries. As a result, such organizations typically suffer from "functional silo syndrome," known to the lay person as bureaucracy. The main difficulty with bureaucracy is that functional managers are given power and independence, and are charged with running their departments without reference to functional interrelationships. These interrelationships are considered the province of top management, whose job it is to "relate" the functions to one another like pieces on a chessboard. (In very large corporations a similar situation often exists at a higher level between divisional managers.)

In a bureaucracy, there are few incentives to share information not perceived by functional managers to be of vital interest outside that specific function—even if the information would benefit the company as a whole were it more widely disseminated. Predictably, bureaucracy makes an organization ignorant and ultimately a little stupid, because even when one function possesses important information, the rest of the organization (usu-

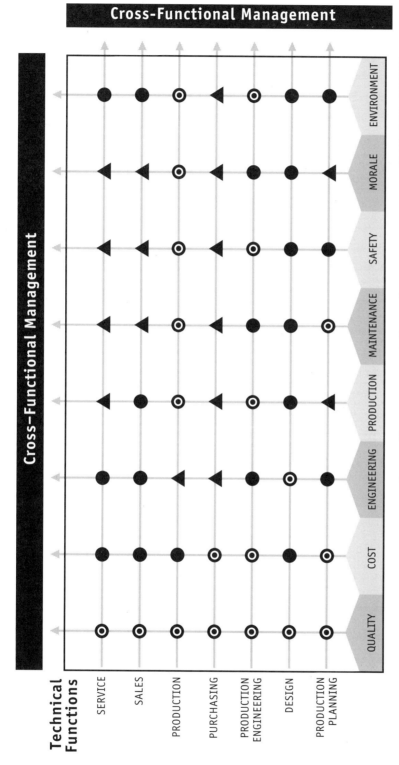

Cross-Functional Management

Cross-Functional Management

Technical Functions

SERVICE
SALES
PRODUCTION
PURCHASING
PRODUCTION ENGINEERING
DESIGN
PRODUCTION PLANNING

QUALITY
COST
ENGINEERING
PRODUCTION
MAINTENANCE
SAFETY
MORALE
ENVIRONMENT

⊙ Strong Relation
● Normal Relation
◀ Weak Relation

Lean Management Functions

Source: Adapted from Kaoru Ishikawa, *What Is Total Quality Control?* (Englewood Cliffs, N.J.: Prentice-Hall, 1985). p. 115.

FIGURE 1-2.
CROSS-FUNCTIONAL MANAGEMENT MATRIX

ally including top management) is left in the dark. Thus the organization as a whole cannot act intelligently.

Strategic planning in mass production organizations often results in plans that are disconnected from a company's true condition and capabilities. Betting on their own careers rather than on the future of the company, managers in function-based organizations tend to withhold information that might reflect poorly on their own performance or prevent approval of a pet project. Consequently, strategic plans may be based more on wishful thinking than on concrete facts. Even a brilliant plan may fail in implementation because the managers charged with fulfilling the plan focus not on overall benefits to the company, but on benefits to themselves.

Cross-functional management solves the problem of bureaucracy by redefining how organizations work. Top management no longer presumes to regulate the minute details of functional interrelationships. Instead, top management identifies issues that require cross-functional communication and cooperation, chooses team members from the functions concerned, gives the teams power to inform and even override departmental decisions (within certain bounds), and charges the teams to act on behalf of the company as a whole.

Throughout the process of strategic planning and implementation, cross-functional management improves both the factual basis of the strategic planning process and the chances of successful implementation of the final plan. Drawn from functional departments across the organization, cross-functional management teams develop, deploy, implement, and verify the annual improvement policy. They focus on company goals, and strive to remove and bypass the formidable obstacles posed by bureaucratic thinking and behavior.

BECOMING A ZERO-WASTE COMPANY

It takes a great amount of dedicated effort to reach level one. What a company will discover when it reaches that level is that it takes an even greater effort to stay lean, because the target itself is constantly changing. What drives companies that maintain their world class status year after year is the goal of going further—of reaching level zero in each key area. Delta Zero is the name we apply to this extreme target and to the spirit or mindset that fuels the effort to reach it. The Delta Zero concept is explained further in Chapter 2.

THE FIRST STEP: RECOGNIZING WASTE

The concept of Delta Zero is related to the pursuit of zero waste. One major reason that companies which have instituted lean production and lean management are so unbeatable is that lean companies pursue zero waste relentlessly in all processes and operations. Most manufacturing operations have a lot of waste that passes unrecognized. To become a zero-waste organization in the spirit of Delta Zero, you must first learn to recognize waste.

Toyota's Taiichi Ohno defined waste as anything in a process that does not add value to a product or service. "Value" is what a well-informed customer would be willing to pay for a perfect product delivered on time. Therefore *anything* in a process that does not contribute to the creation of a perfect product or its timely delivery is *waste.* Ohno identified seven areas where waste lurks:

- *defects*
- *inspection*
- *transportation*
- *motion*
- *overproduction*
- *changeover*
- *inventory*

Within each Toyota factory, transportation patterns, work-motion patterns, production targets, changeover times, and inventory levels were improved, standardized, and controlled over time. This process of waste reduction was accomplished through small group activities using industrial engineering principles and companywide quality control techniques.

Ohno was extremely ambitious. His goal was zero waste in production: zero defects, zero changeover, zero inventory, even zero quality control. Lean management also focuses on removing waste—not only from production, but also from the organization's structure and management practices. In that light, two additional areas of potential waste should be considered:

- *wasted information*
- *lost creative insight*

A company that cannot learn how to tap, gather, share, and process information it possesses and the creative insight that its employees bring to the job is a company that will never reach lean.

THE ZERO-WASTE GOALS

The Lean Management System synthesizes these nine areas of waste into a set of zero-waste goals, one for each of the nine key areas in which the company measures its progress:

1. *Customer focus*	**Zero customer dissatisfaction**
2. *Leadership*	**Zero misalignment**
3. *Lean organization*	**Zero bureaucracy**
4. *Partnering*	**Zero stakeholder dissatisfaction**
5. *Information architecture*	**Zero lost information**
6. *Culture of improvement*	**Zero wasted creativity**
7. *Lean production*	**Zero non-value-adding work**
8. *Lean equipment management*	**Zero failures, zero defects**
9. *Lean engineering*	**Zero lost opportunity**

Later chapters will demonstrate how these elements are used to grow the company through the Lean Management System.

The Lean Radar Chart shown in Figure 1-3 is a device to help companies visualize their baselines and improvement in the nine key areas. As you go through the Lean Management System, you will diagnose your organization's achievement level in each key. You will measure yourself on a scale from five to one, marking your score on the appropriate spoke of the chart. A score of five means your company is still more or less a mass production organization.

After the diagnosis in all nine areas, you connect the dots marked on each spoke to form a polygon that represents the state of your company. The larger the polygon, the further you are from lean. The goal is to become a symmetrical polygon at level one in all nine key areas. Through cycles of innovative business renewal and strategic improvement, a company *learns* its way toward this goal of lean, world class management.

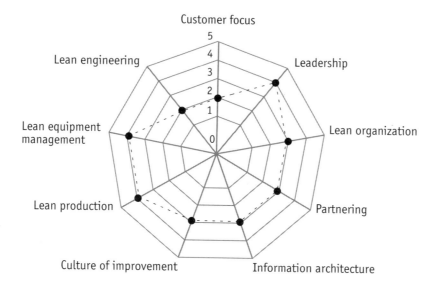

FIGURE 1-3.
THE LEAN RADAR CHART

CONCLUSION

Lean management is a system designed for companies committed to leading the lean production revolution. It is a strategy for managing constant change. Lean management depends on a humanistic approach, an unshakable confidence in the inherent creative spirit residing in each worker, and a firm commitment to promoting their well-being.

The Lean Management System will take time to master. Firms with prior experience in total quality management, JIT, or total productive maintenance—strategies that build effective work cultures—will probably require at least three years for successful implementation. Firms without significant experience will require at least five years to fully implement this system. Firms with fewer than 500 employees may require less time.

The results of implementing a Lean Management System will be dramatic but not necessarily apparent at first. The most important qualities for lean management are patience and a long-term perspective. This kind of thinking, however, does not indulge slowness to act. On the contrary, it requires constant assessment, and constant awareness. Patience means working hard, but not pushing to achieve quick, short-term results. It means allowing the internal logic of lean to take root and grow its course. This is the kind of thinking that will lead to the right growth, to a legacy of which its architects will be proud.

Chapter 2 completes the introduction to the Lean Management System with an overview of the system's main components.

NOTE

1. See James P. Womack, Daniel T. Jones, and Daniel Roos, *The Machine That Changed the World* (New York: Rawson Associates, 1990), 278.

CHAPTER 2

A Lean Management
System Overview

IMPLEMENTING LEAN MANAGEMENT means breaking old patterns and installing new ones. To accomplish this, an organization needs a whole new set of tools and a framework for applying them. It needs a *system*.

The dictionary definition of a system includes the following entries:

- a regularly interacting or interdependent group of items forming a unified whole
- an organized set of doctrines, ideas, or principles
- an organized or established procedure
- a manner of classifying, symbolizing, or schematizing[1]

The Lean Management System captures all of these elements. It merges a strong but flexible conceptual architecture with specific application tools to form an integrated whole that aligns the various parts of an organization to make a change of great magnitude. This chapter presents an overview of the building blocks and tools of the Lean Management System.

The backbone of the Lean Management System is a carefully constructed conceptual architecture that supports the structural, interpersonal, external, and internal relationships governing a company's operations. It has three main elements: the development framework, the Business Renewal Process, and Strategic Improvement Cycles.

THE DEVELOPMENT FRAMEWORK

The development framework comprises several key components:

- Three cornerstones of growth
- Nine keys to development
- Five levels of organizational learning

These structural elements have been developed to refine management's thinking about how to define, build, and manage their organizations. They will be described in detail in this chapter.

The development framework is supported by a Business Renewal Process that creates a long-term Development Plan for the organization, and multiple rounds of the lean management Strategic Improvement Cycle, which turns the Development Plan into action. The steps and phases of these cycles are laid out in full detail in Parts II and III of this book.

The force that animates all of these elements and propels them toward an ideal, waste-free state is Delta Zero.

Three Cornerstones of Growth

The Lean Management System is structured around three necessities of lean production: strategic planning, organizational structure, and human resource capabilities. These three necessities are distilled into a working concept the Lean Management System calls the *three cornerstones of growth,* or *Strategy, Structure,* and *Strengths* (see Figure 2-1). While all companies have these three elements, just as all buildings have a foundation, walls, and infrastructure, a lean company is aware of their existence and features, and will organize its growth around them. A carpenter who knows a building's foundation, material, and structure has much greater success in remodeling than one who doesn't. A lean company that wants to grow must first have a clear sense of its own strategy, structure, and strengths.

Strategy refers to strategic intent—the kind of business the company aims to be—and to a plan of action. The right strategy will match the business's unique strengths with the most valuable customer segments in the right markets, spelling out the development of its structure and strengths

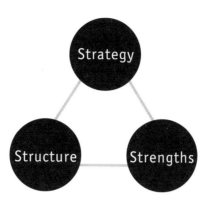

FIGURE 2-1.
THE THREE CORNERSTONES OF GROWTH

over time. The point of all strategic planning is to prepare the business for the future. In a Lean Management System, *customer focus* and *leadership* are key features of a company's strategy.

Structure refers to how the business's internal and external relations are arranged, as well as to the flow of information within the total organization, both internal and external. An appropriate structure ensures that the individuals and institutions involved in product development, production, and distribution will communicate and cooperate efficiently and flexibly. In a lean company, *lean organization, partnering,* and *information architecture* hold up this second growth cornerstone.

Strengths refers to organizational capabilities or step-by-step production and support routines mastered by the company, through which it gets work done. The appropriate mix of strengths ensures that strategy can be executed and a broad range of structural possibilities expressed. The right strengths ensure a readiness and responsiveness to changes in the competitive environment, whether anticipated or sudden. A company's *improvement culture, production system, equipment management,* and *engineering* control its strengths.

Nine Keys to Development

Managing strategy, structure, and strengths is easier said than done, especially under conditions of rapid change. In mass production organizations, strategy, structure, and strengths are products of past development processes based on old assumptions about the future. Without a correct and

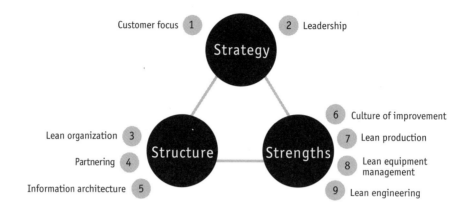

FIGURE 2-2.
THE NINE KEYS TO DEVELOPMENT

clear view of the future, change can disconnect a firm's strategy, structure, and strengths, spinning a company into organizational turmoil. More often than not, old-style business leaders concentrate narrowly on financial aspects of strategy, failing to consider the company's structure or strengths. What frequently results is a disconnected strategy with an outmoded structure and inadequate operational strengths.

To ensure a more holistic approach to development of policy, the Lean Management System has developed a flexible and controlled response to change through what we call the nine keys to development. Each key (italicized in the previous section) regulates one of the growth cornerstones—Strategy, Structure, or Strengths (see Figure 2-2), and, as mentioned in Chapter 1, each key is associated with a particular zero-waste goal. As later chapters will show, these keys form the main categories in which an organization charts its progress. A drive to build or improve the nine keys distinguishes a lean from a mass producer. Implementers should note that these keys are not set in stone; we expect that our own system will continue to evolve and that implementers will sometimes develop new keys to meet their own particular needs.

The Keys to Strategy. The two keys to building an effective strategy are customer focus and leadership. Mastery of these keys will keep a company from being blindsided by unexpected customer demands and failing to develop capabilities to satisfy new demands.

KEY 1.   ***Customer focus*** refers to feedback processing methods that inform a company what the customer wants and ensure that it is delivered. When the customer dreams of something, the company will know it and—if all other keys are in top gear—the customer will get it. Since customer satisfaction is the straightest road to profit, its impact on profitability is direct. The impact of this key penetrates an entire business, from design to production to delivery. *Goal: zero customer dissatisfaction.*

KEY 2.   ***Leadership*** is the management team's ability to translate customer requirements into concrete policies, organizational structures, and production strengths. This key's relationship to profit is critical, as illustrated by the way leadership, in providing direction and support for overall company development, improves cost, quality, and speed. *Goal: zero misalignment between strategy and human resources.*

The Keys to Structure. Mastering these structural keys will ensure a flat, team-based organization that is well integrated with suppliers and the environment, and in which vital information is always available at the point of use.

KEY 3.   ***Lean organization*** is the structure of interlocking teams required to eliminate bureaucracy, minimize overhead, and promote responsiveness to market conditions. *Goal: zero bureaucracy.*

KEY 4.   ***Partnering*** is a set of cooperative, trust-based relationships that must be effectively deployed to all stakeholders—employees, suppliers, and society at large—to remain competitive. *Goal: zero stakeholder dissatisfaction.*

KEY 5.   ***Information architecture*** structures the creation and distribution of information into a framework that supports a team-based organization. Architectural features include improvement-oriented performance measures and management accounting systems as well as the use of visual control techniques. *Goal: zero lost information.*

Key	Zero-Waste Goal	Relation to Profit
1. Customer focus	Zero customer dissatisfaction	Customer input and feedback assures quality. Customer satisfaction supports sales.
2. Leadership	Zero misalignment	Direction and support for development improves cost, quality, and speed.
3. Lean organization	Zero bureaucracy	Team-based operations reduce overhead by eliminating bureaucracy and ensuring information flow and cooperation.
4. Partnering	Zero stakeholder dissatisfaction	Flexible relationships with suppliers, distributors, and society improve quality, cost, and speed.
5. Information architecture	Zero lost information	Knowledge required for operations is accurate and timely, thus improving quality, cost, and speed.
6. Culture of improvement	Zero wasted creativity	Employee participation in eliminating operations waste improves cost, quality, and speed.
7. Lean production	Zero non-value-adding work	Total employee involvement and aggressive waste elimination promote speedier operations and eradicate inventories.
8. Lean equipment management	Zero failures, zero defects	Longer equipment life and design improvement reduce cost. Meticulous maintenance and equipment improvement increase quality. Absolute availability and efficiency increase speed.
9. Lean engineering	Zero lost opportunity	Early resolution of design problems with customers and suppliers significantly reduces cost, while improving quality and cycle time.

FIGURE 2-3.
HOW THE NINE KEYS IMPROVE PROFITABILITY

The Keys to Strength. The keys to strength will ensure a workforce capable of improving any process and create a flexible production system; so that when the customer dreams of something new, the organization can deliver it in minimal time.

KEY 6.   *Culture of improvement* equips teams and individual employees to analyze strategic gaps and quality problems to find root causes, and then conceive, implement, and standardize effective solutions. *Goal: zero wasted creativity.*

KEY 7.   *Lean production* includes the array of waste-reduction techniques such as quick changeover, JIT production methods, mistake-proofing, and other methods that help companies produce exactly what the customer wants, when it is wanted. *Goal: zero non-value-adding work.*

KEY 8.   **Lean equipment management** refers to a total productive maintenance (TPM) approach that ensures the efficiency, accuracy, and ease of operation and maintenance, as well as readiness and availability of equipment and systems. *Goal: zero failures, zero defects.*

KEY 9.   **Lean engineering** refers to the practice of concurrent engineering and all necessary means to rapidly and consistently design and produce new products that delight customers. *Goal: zero lost opportunity.*

Figure 2-3 summarizes how the keys and their zero-waste goals improve profitability.

Five Levels of Organizational Learning

What can't be measured can't be controlled. Tracking the progress in the nine keys requires a system of measurement. The Lean Management System establishes ascending criteria for each key that help you evaluate your organization's progress toward world class competitiveness. The Lean Management System divides the progression of development from a mass production organization to a lean one into five distinct levels of organizational learning:

LEVEL FIVE   *Mass production*
LEVEL FOUR   *System initiation*
LEVEL THREE   *System development*
LEVEL TWO   *System maturity*
LEVEL ONE   *System excellence*

By definition lean management can never be truly mastered. A true world class competitor will always strive to improve, refine, and surpass today's achievements. The zero-waste goal target in each key area is continuously moving beyond one's grasp.

In each of the nine key areas, learning begins with a self-assessment of current conditions. A company that diagnoses itself as a mass production organization will strive to initialize lean management through focused pilot projects in critical operational areas. Having accomplished this task, management may reassess the company as a level four organization. Ascending to the next level requires the company to take what it has learned from its pilot projects and deploy it to all major operational areas, the successful completion of which will project the organization to level three lean status. The firm may next face the challenge of extending the new practices into all areas of operations, including support. Ascending to level two (system maturity) requires more skill than all previous efforts combined.

Success is defined as having achieved at least level three (system development) in all nine keys. Development from level five to level three can be fairly rapid in all keys; development from level three to levels two and one is much slower. Company size and other factors may affect the rate of development. Firms already far along in implementing various keys will require less time.

Once Lean Management Systems are fully matured at level two, graduation to world class competitor level requires the greatest effort of all. A notoriously tough college professor was once asked by a nervous student what it would take to earn an "A" in his class. The professor, peering over his glasses, replied, "To earn an 'A' in my class, *you* have to teach *me* something." To reach level one in any of the nine keys, a company must be in the forefront of best practice. It must demonstrate refinement and originality, and provide a benchmark for other companies to follow. The Lean Management System can help a firm reach this state, but everyone in the organization must be prepared for a lot of hard work.

Development through the five levels is not always a smooth climb. The nine keys are linked in a single system: just as improvement in one key enables better performance in all others, poor performance in one key will hinder better performance in all others. Companies just starting on the path to lean production and lean management often realize for the first time how uneven their previous development has been. Many companies find that they have overdeveloped their engineering capabilities and underdeveloped their cultural and production capabilities.

It is virtually impossible for a company to develop each key with equally high investments of attention and intensity. Emphasizing two or three keys each year as focal areas for the company's improvement energy is what grows a company from year to year. In the Lean Management System, these two or three keys are referred to as *critical keys*. They are not necessarily the keys that are most important to the company's long-term strategy, but rather the ones that most need improvement to support progress in the others. These critical keys will shift from year to year depending on the company's focus during each strategic planning cycle. Identifying different critical keys each year adjusts the balance among strategy, structure, and strengths, and controls the rate and direction of the company's evolution.

Development can be controlled, but it often proceeds more slowly than we wish. Installing lean management technology is not like plugging in a machine and flicking the "on" switch. It is based on people, teamwork, and total employee involvement, and it requires time to implement, mature, and refine.

THE BUSINESS RENEWAL PROCESS

Lean companies reexamine their reason for existence on a regular basis and infuse the entire organization with the answer they develop. A lean company involves its entire workforce in continuously reengineering its production processes and ultimately redefines the industry by the way it does things. Such cultures of improvement encourage quantum leaps in improvement innovation. Toyota's invention of just-in-time production was just such a leap. The attitude of improvement so permeates lean companies today that quantum leaps are a regular occurrence. Toyota's development of the Lexus, a new standard in the luxury car market, is a case in point. A Lexus costs 15 to 30 percent less to manufacture than a comparable Mercedes-Benz. Hewlett-Packard's phenomenal printer business is another example of a quantum leap that redefined the industry. Through a combination of technical innovation and drastic cost reduction, HP now dominates the market for personal ink-jet and laser printers.

Lean producers not only reengineer their production processes, they redesign, reinvent, and reengineer entire businesses on a schedule. Using breakthrough thinking, lean companies compete on the basis of surprise, by creating a stream of new product and production standards for their competitors. The process through which lean companies create the future is called the *Business Renewal Process* (see Figure 2-4). It requires a company to start with a blank slate periodically, and ask: Why are we in business at all?

Establishing a Vision	Building a Development Strategy
• Envision the future • Analyze core capabilities • Revise the vision • Deploy the vision	• Conduct a Corporate Diagnosis • Review strategic information • Define strategic keys • Produce a Development Plan

FIGURE 2-4.
THE BUSINESS RENEWAL PROCESS

The process of business renewal, described in detail in Chapters 3 and 4, is closely related to traditional strategic planning. Using market forecasts, traditional strategic planning tries to ensure greater profits or stock prices by defining a product's variety, quality, markets, distribution, and prices. The Business Renewal Process continues these mainstays of traditional strategic planning, but also incorporates some innovations.

- First, the lean management Business Renewal Process is repeated whenever it's required, but at least every three to five years. This conscious decision to renew the organization's focus ensures that a company keeps pace with the shifting business climate—that is, changes in technology, best practices, and market conditions.
- Second, the first step in the Business Renewal Process is to define a far-reaching vision that focuses sharply on customers' needs and desires. The starting point is vision, rather than profit, because profit is merely a by-product of customer satisfaction. Profit analysis, though important, plays a secondary role.

- Third, Business Renewal Process requires corporate management to generate a lean management Development Plan based on the nine keys. This will help build new organizational structures and strengths to match new visions and strategies.

THE STRATEGIC IMPROVEMENT CYCLE

The Business Renewal Process is followed by several rounds of learning and improvement called *Strategic Improvement Cycles*. These annual or semi-annual cycles are the basis of the "policy bridge" between management's vision and the specifics of implementation. Each cycle attacks specific areas that need attention, enabling a company to progress from one level of organizational excellence to the next. By undergoing this process, the firm gradually will realize or come closer to its vision.

The strategic improvement cycle has four distinct phases (see Figure 2-5):

PHASE I. *Focus.* In this phase, a top management team devises an annual policy that focuses on improving two or three of the key areas. This policy helps the company concentrate its energies on closing critical strategic gaps.

PHASE II. *Standardization.* This phase standardizes policy, first, by deploying it to all managers, supervisors, and team leaders, and second, by involving all employees in its implementation through focused team activities and documentation.

PHASE III. *Adherence.* This phase assures the company's adherence to its annual policy through a system of concise reports and an annual top management audit, described in detail in the companion volume, *Corporate Diagnosis*.

PHASE IV. *Reflection.* In Phase IV, the top management team analyzes performance for the previous period and reviews the company's capabilities, markets, and industry conditions. Based on this, it prioritizes problems and strategic challenges to address, then revises the annual policy in preparation for another cycle of improvement.

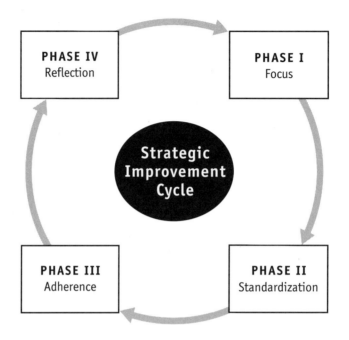

FIGURE 2-5.
THE STRATEGIC IMPROVEMENT CYCLE

These phases, treated in depth in Chapters 5 through 8, help a company assess its direction, learn from its mistakes, and build competitive strengths for success in the future. Each phase of the cycle involves processes that help teams prioritize and analyze problems, and then develop, prioritize, and implement improvement ideas to achieve the organization's strategic goals.

The company repeats this cycle until it reaches a certain level of improvement, then commences another Business Renewal Process. Figure 2-6 depicts how these cycles flow together in a spiral of improvement.

Normally, the Strategic Improvement Cycle is repeated once a year. Companies just beginning lean management may take up to 18 months to complete a cycle. Others operating in fast-moving markets may repeat the cycle twice within a year to accelerate organizational learning.

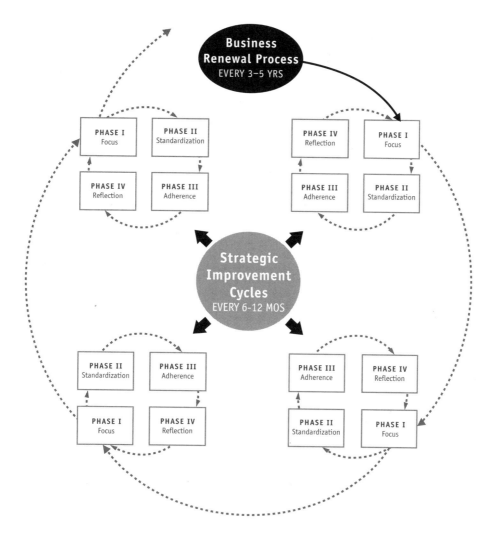

FIGURE 2-6.
A GRAPHIC MODEL OF THE BUSINESS RENEWAL PROCESS AND
STRATEGIC IMPROVEMENT CYCLES

DELTA ZERO

As mentioned in Chapter 1, lean companies owe their success in part to maintaining zero waste in operations. Lean companies are unbeatable not merely because they are waste free, but also because they expect the unexpected, and meet each new challenge with moves unexpected by customers and competitors. Lean companies are innovative, flexible, agile. Being so far beyond their competitors' capabilities, the activities of lean companies are almost invisible to their contenders. When American manufacturers visited Japanese factories in the late 1970s, they literally could not see what was taking place before their eyes. Since these Western visitors did not know what to look for, innovations that could return billions of dollars in profit went unnoticed, even as they stared them in the face. The new techniques of management such as JIT and TPM sprang at them seemingly from nowhere. Likewise, competitors of lean organizations literally don't know where lean companies are coming from; it is as if these lean companies had disappeared into thin air, only to spring out when the time is right, with devastating effect. This ability to surprise is one small facet of the power of Delta Zero.

Delta Zero is the union of two concepts: *delta,* the Greek letter symbolizing incremental change, and *zero,* the Arabic numeral symbolizing void.

DELTA ZERO

Essentially, Delta Zero refers to the paradox of learning. All learning, personal as well as organizational, takes place on one of two levels:

- *Normal learning,* in which we add knowledge or increase performance incrementally within paradigms—fundamental structures of information that define the boundaries and structure of the various spheres in which we operate.
- *Paradigmatic learning,* in which we create new paradigms.

Without paradigms, our minds would be simply overwhelmed by the flood of information coming from our senses. Paradigms establish familiar mental norms we often take for granted. We usually do not question the paradigm in which our view of the universe is grounded; we merely extend or embellish that view. *Delta* is a good symbol for the structured learning that takes place within a normal, accepted paradigm.

A change in paradigm is always revolutionary, starting anew with a clean slate. Consider the development of new paradigms in science. Examples include Copernicus's idea that the planets revolve around the sun, Newton's discovery of the laws of motion and gravitation, and Einstein's theory of relativity. Like a baseline, *Zero* represents the creative force that stimulates new paradigms to emerge.

The two types of learning, normal and paradigmatic, are often in conflict. Old paradigms die hard. Because they affect so much of what we know and do, new paradigms are challenged simply in the interest of truth. Einstein's theory of relativity was not generally accepted until scientific observation confirmed several of the theory's predictions. Toyota's production system is only now spreading widely, after the sustained performance of Toyota and other lean companies has proved it beyond doubt. Moreover, people engaged in normal learning within an old paradigm often resist a new paradigm, even with clear evidence of validity, because change requires effort, or because they have vested interests in the old paradigm. Scientists sometimes resist new ideas because they can make old research (and reputations) obsolete. Within the business world, managers may resist new approaches because they imply change in organizational structure and loss of power.

For an organization to grow through learning, managers must grasp both the Delta—normal organizational learning—and the Zero—paradigmatic organizational learning. Managers must encourage learning through existing paradigms of the customer and the process while also preparing for business renewal and the adoption of new ideas. Because of the established nature of normal learning, new ideas frequently come from the fringes of the organization, or even from outside it.

The concept of Delta Zero is intended to ground management in both normal and paradigmatic learning simultaneously. Leaders must manage their paradigms to promote learning within the existing paradigm, to look out for valid new paradigms that will enhance organizational knowledge and competitiveness, and to manage the inevitable tension between the two approaches so that entrenched ideas do not stifle growth.

Delta Zero is both a principle and an attitude. As a principle, Delta Zero is a reminder that all things are in constant flux. Change is a given. A company that anticipates change from unexpected directions is a company that can transform itself to the reality of the changed environment. A company that clings to how it *wishes,* hopes, or erroneously imagines its future environment to be will be uprooted, broken, or at least badly shaken. Successful companies that remain steadfast through time and variable conditions are usually lean. The Lean Management System is about molding your company so that it has the sensors to see change, the flexibility to accept it, and the resources to survive it.

As an attitude, Delta Zero supports the ultimate purpose of the Lean Management System: growing a blue chip company. This program is not for those wanting to reap quick riches from a source that will disappear with the next economic cycle. The Lean Management System is for companies with a commitment to building a source of high and steady income over the long term. It's about building a legacy for the future. Most important, it's about building your own personal commitment to growth.

THE LEAN MANAGEMENT TOOLS

Leadership and instruction can cut a path to lean management, but to make the going less bumpy, there are special tools to smooth the way. After it absorbs the components of the conceptual tools, a budding lean system requires physical tools for team-based implementation of lean management. These physical tools are described as follows.

Corporate Diagnosis: Meeting Global Standards for Excellence

Corporate Diagnosis, the companion volume to this work, is designed to support the hands-on approach to diagnosis described in Chapters 4 and 7. To determine how well a company is meeting its strategic targets, diagnostic teams visit each department and section to learn from middle managers, supervisors, and employees the firm's weaknesses and strengths. *Corporate Diagnosis* provides model questions and a five-level scoring system to gauge a company's progress. In addition, criteria for the world's top business prizes—the Malcolm Baldrige National Quality Award, the Shingo Prize for Manufacturing Excellence, the Deming Application Prize, and the PM Prize for Total Productive Maintenance—are presented alongside the nine keys of the Lean Management System to facilitate integration with these popular guidelines. Using *Corporate Diagnosis,* managers can benchmark their company against recognized international standards of excellence.

Lean Management Forms

Lean management relies on an integrated system of forms to facilitate team interaction and track progress through the strategic improvement cycle (see Figure 2-7 for examples). Use of the appropriate forms actually drives deployment and implementation of the annual policy. Having appropriate forms and knowing how to use them can mean the difference between a strong plan's successful implementation or disappointing failure.

This book uses a detailed case study to show how the forms are used and how they work together to support team-based operations and total involvement. Using the forms, managers and employees can document the phases of each Strategic Improvement Cycle, track the details of progress, and organize supporting information. The forms also promote autonomous improvement activity in the office or on the shop floor, helping middle managers and team leaders in setting monthly and daily improvement priorities in regular meetings with frontline teams. These forms include reporting procedures to facilitate regular review and feedback. Readers can obtain blank versions of prepared forms from the publisher, or can create their own to suit their situation.

Lean Management Wall Charts

Lean management is aided by the use of large wall charts to define and facilitate the cross-functional team relationships that drive the lean management process. These wall charts promote team-based discussion and decision-making. The Workcenter Control Board shown in Figure 2-8, for example, communicates vital information about important activities to all employees simply and effectively. Introducing this chart to all areas of the company provides all the information managers and teams need to skillfully manage and execute strategic priorities on a daily basis. Blank versions of these charts are available from the publisher.

This completes Part I of the book. Parts II and III will guide the reader through an entire Lean Management System planning and improvement cycle from start to finish, illustrating the instruction with a case study based on a successful implementation.

NOTE

1. *Merriam-Webster's Collegiate Dictionary*, 10th ed. (Springfield, Mass.: Merriam Webster, 1993).

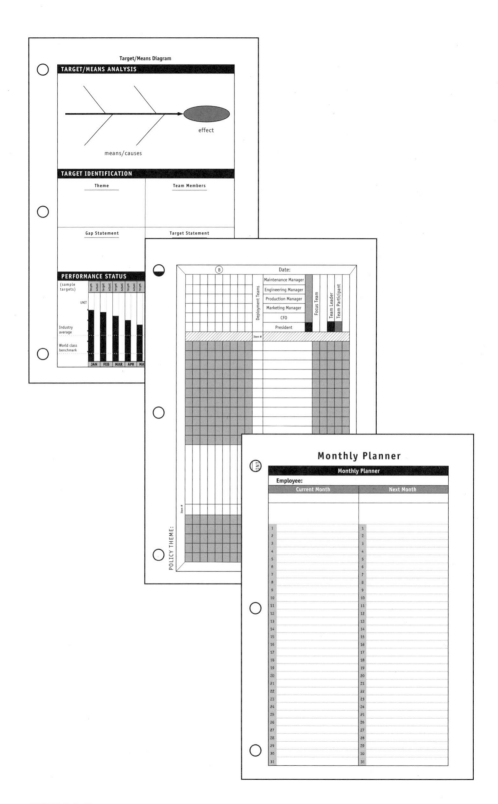

FIGURE 2-7.
LEAN MANAGEMENT FORMS

Implementation Plan
Theme: Cost Down, Competitiveness Up!
Date:

Department: Production
Work Area: Workcenter 1
Area Manager: Production coordinator

Nonesuch Casting Company

Critical Key	Control/Check	#	Owner	Strategy	Target	Actual	Start	Complete	1	2	3	4	5	6	7	8	9	10	11	12
																				MONTH
Leadership	Adherence	2.4	**Production mgr.**																	
		2.4.1	Production coord.	Monthly review																
			Team leader 1																	
			Team leader 2																	
			Team leader 3																	
			Team leader 4																	
			Team leader 5																	
		2.4.2	Production coord.																	
			Team leader 1																	
Lean equip. mgt.	Equip./process impr.	8.1	**Eng. manager**	Total Prod. Maint.																
	Availability	8.1.1																		
	Changeover time	8.1.1b	Production coord.	Adopt SMED																
			Team leader 1																	
			Team leader 2																	
			Team leader 5																	
	Performance efficiency	8.1.2																		
	Minor stoppages	8.1.2a	Production coord.																	
			Team leader 2																	
			Team leader 3																	
			Team leader 4																	
	Autonomous maint.	8.2	**Production mgr.**	Autonomous maint.																
	Initial cleaning	8.2.1	Production coord.	....																
			Team leader 1																	
			Team leader 2																	
	Sources of dirt	8.2.2	Production coord.	....																
			Team leader 1																	
			Team leader 2																	
	Establish standards	8.3.2	Production coord.	....																
			Team leader 1																	
	Safety	8.3	**Production mgr.**	DuPont program																
	Initial audit	8.3.1	Production coord.	....																
			Team leader 1																	
			Team leader 2																	
			Team leader 3																	
			Team leader 4																	
	Establish standards	8.3.2																		
			Team leader 1																	
			Team leader 2																	
			Team leader 3																	
			Team leader 4																	

FIGURE 2-8.
WORKCENTER CONTROL BOARD

PART II

The Business Renewal Process

It is a bad plan that admits of no modification.
—Publius Syrus

TO COMPETE IN A MARKET DEFINED BY LEAN PRODUCTION, a company needs to ground itself in the attitude of Delta Zero and renew its Strategy, Structure, and Strengths on a regular basis. In Part II, we define a process of business renewal, which begins with a far-reaching vision that redefines what the company will be in the long term, and ends with the creation of a strategic development plan for building new structures and strengths.

Traditional strategic planning techniques often focus on profit as the means to company growth. By beginning with vision, business renewal recognizes profit as a result, a by-product of growth, and customer satisfaction as the means. Attributing productivity to machines rather than to methods and human relations, strategic planners in mass production organizations tend to ignore the need to plan for organizational and human development. But quality, speed, and flexibility in production systems are not assured by equipment alone; they must be built upon cooperative team-based structures and upgraded human capabilities. With the advent of lean production, developmental planning has become more important than planning for new technological hardware.

Throughout this part, we assume that the reader's organization has a traditional strategic planning mechanism. It is necessary, after all, to define products, markets, distribution channels, and prices, and some of this data feeds into the steps of business renewal planning. Because so much has been written about strategic planning, however,[1] we will focus primarily on the differences between business renewal and traditional strategic planning.

The purpose of the Business Renewal Process is to develop two things: a company vision for the next three to five years and a concrete development plan based on this vision. In addition, this phase of work also discovers and determines a baseline—a Zero—upon which to measure future improvements and a set of strategic keys on which long-term success rests. The renewal team that will work on this cycle consists primarily of the company's top management.

The Business Renewal Process has eight steps:

1. Envision the future	5. Conduct a Corporate Diagnosis
2. Analyze core capabilities	6. Review strategic information
3. Revise the vision	7. Define strategic keys
4. Deploy the vision	8. Produce a Development Plan

Chapter 3 describes the first four steps, building the company vision. The last four steps, presented in Chapter 4, deal with the building of a development strategy.

Coming up with a vision and a strategic plan that will guide and motivate a company to a position of strength for the next Business Renewal Process requires tremendous thought and research by its top management. Gathering information about industry-affecting factors and thoroughly researching projections in spheres potentially affecting your business is no small task. Following the steps laid out in this part should help minimize the disarray and confusion that often surround this phase of growth.

Introducing the Nonesuch Casting Company Case

The Lean Management System is an idealized system. Most companies that adopt it will customize it to suit themselves. However, a good manual gives examples to help the reader accomplish prescribed steps with assurance. To show how a Lean Management System knits a company together from top to bottom and across functional lines, we offer a case study of the Nonesuch Casting Company, a fictional case based on an actual manufacturing company's experience planning and implementing a major change initiative. All of the charts and forms prescribed in Parts II and III of this book have been filled in with information pertaining to Nonesuch Casting. Although the example is based largely on real situations, facts have been modified to serve the purposes of illustration. Basic background on the Nonesuch Company appears in the box.

About Nonesuch Casting Company

Established in 1982, Nonesuch is a small manufacturer of aluminum casting located in an isolated rural area. A union shop employing 150 people on three shifts per day, Nonesuch produces two million cast aluminum pieces a year from its single plant. The casting company was originally built to serve a sister plant, a nearby automobile factory operated by their parent corporation, the Nonesuch Automobile Corporation. The last recession forced the local sister plant to close, at which time the CEO of Nonesuch Casting learned that his company could not stay in business unless it became a world class competitor. The Nonesuch Automobile Corporation promised to continue buying from Nonesuch Casting, but only if their products could meet the parent company's high standards for quality, cost, and delivery.

Since the nearest automobile plant was located thousands of miles away, cost and delivery standards would be extremely difficult to meet. While not exactly inferior, plant operations at Nonesuch Casting could certainly not compare to the best in the world. Being so distant from its primary markets, Nonesuch could not compete based on location. The company had only one option: it would have to achieve and maintain *exceptional* quality levels while simultaneously reducing costs. Traditional management methods could not accomplish this. It became clear that the Nonesuch Casting Company would have to do whatever it took to implement some version of lean production.

NOTE

1. Sources that provide useful background reading on traditional strategic planning and analysis include Kenichi Ohmae, *The Mind of the Strategist* (New York: McGraw-Hill, 1982); Henry Mintzberg, *The Rise and Fall of Strategic Planning* (New York: Prentice Hall, 1994); J. I. Moore, *Writers on Strategy and Strategic Management* (London: Penguin, 1992).

CHAPTER 3

Establishing a Vision

WHAT IS VISION? In dynamic business organizations, a vision helps a firm accomplish two tasks vital for lean functions. Vision establishes a strategic intent. And vision creates companywide alignment—a prerequisite for sustaining a team-based culture for analysis, communication, and action. An effective vision states what is important and different about the company, while suggesting a compelling story of growth that inspires the entire workforce to transform their own jobs, eventually transforming the entire company.

The purpose of the company's vision is to establish a strategic intent, and this is a first priority. Once accomplished, the vision instantly proclaims the company's direction of growth. Establishing a vision for a company is not unlike a strategic planning exercise. Top management must first consider its desired business environments and capabilities, along with the existing technological, economic, and social environments in which the company will compete. But unlike a strategy, a company vision establishes a myth for the future around which a company culture may flourish.

A vision helps a company respond effectively to sudden changes by unifying everyone's thinking about its competitive challenges and strategic priorities. A clear vision coordinates the thoughts and actions of all employees since they will all be reading the same script. A concise vision, therefore, is a key element of strategic alignment, forging a creative employee community. As employees communicate and cooperate to establish and reach common goals, they will constantly refer to the company's vision as a guidepost and gradually internalize it into their daily frame of reference.

Vision, a company's ultimate performance standard, is established in four steps:

1. Envision the future
2. Analyze core capabilities
3. Revise the vision
4. Deploy the vision

STEP 1. ENVISION THE FUTURE

The vision that comes out of this business renewal phase is not the vision for a single division, department, or section, but for the entire company. Because this vision will set the tone for growth activities and focus the company's capabilities for the next three to five years, it must be crafted with considerable thought and attention.

The process of vision building described in this chapter is usually carried out by a *renewal team* made up of the company's top corporate management—the CEO or president and his or her direct reports. If this group has more than 12 people, it will be more effective to form a smaller task force to perform the first step: composing a preliminary vision statement in 25 or fewer words. This "trial" vision should express a strategic intent for the firm, but it also must have emotional content—it must create an appealing and plausible myth of the future, one in which all stakeholders will want to take part. A good vision statement will answer the following questions: Who will the company's customers be in ten years? In twenty years? How will they live and work? How will their needs change? What should the company be to serve those needs? An imaginative, bold, and appealing vision will help visualize the company's future products, services, and ability to serve customers.

The renewal team (or the smaller vision task force) should consider how employees and all stakeholders will use this vision to shape their thoughts and communications about the company. Does the vision make sense? Is it exciting? Will people want to be part of this picture of the future? The vision must not only make sense but stimulate excitement and participation.

The process of distilling a good vision from its raw, preliminary form requires rounds of discussion, analysis, and refinement. After agreeing on the preliminary vision, the renewal team invites others to participate in the visioning process, beginning with the full top management team. Other interested parties whose inputs should be sought include representatives from each stakeholder group—board members, employees at all levels, customers, stockholders, suppliers, and government agencies with which the company works closely. If company activities impact their immediate surroundings, this circle of stakeholders should also include representatives from local communities and special interest groups. These parties don't necessarily attend the renewal team's meeting, but they should be consulted for their opinions. Techniques such as focus groups, questionnaires, and live or taped interviews can aid in the gathering of input and feedback.

The Nonesuch Company's renewal team came up with this first draft of their vision statement:

> To Be the Best, Fastest, and Most Profitable
> Aluminum Casting Company in the World.

While not all team members were thoroughly satisfied with this preliminary vision, everyone agreed that it was a good statement with which to begin the discussion.

STEP 2. ANALYZE CORE CAPABILITIES

A clear vision requires a thorough understanding of what the business does well. A vision should be framed in terms of the core capabilities that make up its portfolio of competitive advantages. A core capability is any value-adding activity or competently performed value delivery process that differentiates the firm from its competitors.

This and subsequent vision-building steps should involve the entire top management team, even if a smaller task force carried out the first step. The team should focus on the two or three capabilities your company performs exceptionally well. Highly successful organizations tend to be strongly focused. Toyota, for example, has established a dominant position in the automobile industry by focusing on its production system. Hewlett-Packard focuses on new product development. Traditional strategic analysis and planning activities on an ongoing basis should keep top management aware of the company's capabilities and trends in the market. Consider long-term competitive trends, as well as the technological, political, social, economic, and cultural environments. Don't get weighed down in heavy quantitative modeling, however; keep analysis informal and conversational.

Initial review of information and discussions among the renewal team at Nonesuch led to the conclusion that Nonesuch should focus on its capability in the concurrent engineering of high tech, precision castings.

STEP 3. REVISE THE VISION

After completing preparatory discussions, the renewal team should review the preliminary vision statement. Each team member then writes his or her comments, criticisms, and new vision ideas on Post-its™ and arranges them on a wall or a flip chart. The discussion should continue until the team has fully explored the strengths and weaknesses of the preliminary statement and each member has expressed his or her own vision for the future of the company. Enlisting an outside facilitator to run this meeting provides an impartial moderator for the discussion, allowing members to participate fully without stepping in and out of the facilitator role.

Next, the team applies the affinity diagram technique to categorize its ideas, sorting the Post-its into groups of related topics. The facilitator writes a header card summarizing the ideas of each group. During a break, one of the team members drafts a vision statement addressing the points summarized by the header cards. When the team returns from break, copies of the new composite vision statement are handed out and team members are invited to mark it up. The facilitator creates a third version of the vision statement after reviewing the team's comments.

Recall the preliminary vision statement of the Nonesuch Company's renewal team. After brainstorming ideas for revising the original statement, the Nonesuch management team created the affinity diagram shown in Figure 3-1. Note the header cards that summarize the content of each group of Post-its.

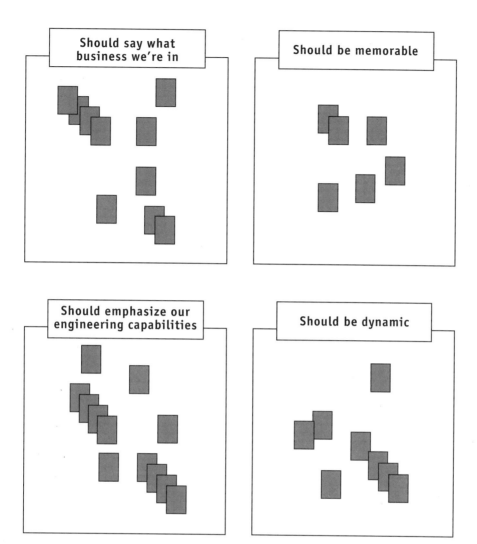

FIGURE 3-1.
SHAPING THE VISION USING AN AFFINITY DIAGRAM

The Nonesuch renewal team felt that the preliminary vision statement was not dynamic and furthermore did not express their customer focus or their core capabilities. After the team completed the affinity diagram and discussed the composite vision that resulted, the facilitator wrote up a new vision statement:

Casting imaginative solutions for a fast-changing world.

This vision was accepted by all the renewal team members.

STEP 4. DEPLOY THE VISION

The CEO announces the new vision statement to the entire company. Then management systematically broadcasts it to the firm's stakeholders across all available media as frequently as possible. The purpose is to instill the new vision into the hearts, minds, and actions of all the stakeholders who influenced it and whose participation is required to implement it. Bill Christopher puts it nicely:

> Once created, the Company Vision becomes its banner, a symbol setting direction for the future. The Vision Statement needs to be seen everywhere, all the time. It will be in company publications, on plaques and displays, on bulletin boards, in management reports, in stockholder reports and financial statements, in project proposals and requests for expenditure, in budgets and plans, in policy manuals and included in work standards—in all places that are seen by company members in their daily work, and by other company constituencies in their contacts with the company. . . . All the time. Everywhere that words appear, there also will appear the Company Vision. On signs. On paper. On computer screens. On PA systems and telecommunications. Everywhere.[1]

The Nonesuch Company used many of these vehicles to spread the company vision. Employees received pens, caps, and pocket-sized cards with the vision statement printed on them, and it appeared on stationery and documents.

With the vision-building portion of business renewal completed, the company is ready to work on its business development strategy.

NOTE

1. William F. Christopher, *Vision, Mission, Total Quality: Leadership Tools for Turbulent Times* (Portland, Ore.: Productivity Press, 1994), p. 10.

CHAPTER 4

Building a
Development Strategy

STRATEGY DOES THREE THINGS: It tells you where you are, where you want to go, and how you can get there.

A strategy is a plan elaborating the steps necessary to achieve a vision. Without these steps, the vision dissipates to mere wishful thinking. The traditional method of devising strategy adds specific targets and timetables to a company's vision, defining the products, markets, distribution channels, and final prices. The lean method for defining strategy also incorporates a long-range development plan for developing the company's three cornerstones—strategy, structure, strengths—based on one or several of the nine keys to development introduced in Chapter 2. The goal of strategy in a lean organization is to provide the right direction, organization, and technical and human resources to satisfy future customer demand. The development plan that results from Lean Management System strategic planning guides the activities of the Strategic Improvement Cycles.

The top management renewal team reconvenes to determine its development strategy after the company has had a chance to digest its new vision. Developmental planning retraces the steps previously taken to create vision, but in much greater detail. The development strategy is built in four steps:

STEP 5. CONDUCT CORPORATE DIAGNOSIS

The introductory chapters mentioned the Corporate Diagnosis as a major element of the Lean Management System. Step 5 of the Business Renewal Process is the first point when it is applied. The diagnosis is used again as a follow-up check during the adherence phase of the Strategic Improvement Cycle. Since the method and forms for this audit are covered thoroughly in the companion *Corporate Diagnosis* volume, we will touch on only its basic elements here.

The Corporate Diagnosis is a method for helping top management understand the company's level of attainment in the nine keys of lean management development. The knowledge gained through this approach supplements the executives' general understanding of the company's core capabilities. It clarifies areas of strength, as well as weaknesses that must be addressed to succeed at lean management. The nine keys provide a structured system for analyzing which of the company's capabilities might provide a basis for competition in markets. A company need not excel in all nine keys simultaneously. In the long term the company will focus on developing inherent strengths in a few strategic competitive keys, and for each annual improvement cycle it will select two or three *critical* keys as the targets for its focused efforts. The first diagnosis serves as a baseline for later rounds of improvement.

Corporate Diagnosis uses a series of questionnaires, one for each of the nine keys. We have developed a set of control points for each key to represent the essential processes and activities required for lean management success. Like the nine keys themselves, these control points are not a closed set; users may want to develop their own specialized control points. From these control points emerge the questions management will use to assess the company's initial status (and later progress) in lean management. Figure 4-1 shows a Lean Management Scoreboard that lists the control points and

CORNER-STONES OF GROWTH	KEYS TO DEVELOPMENT	CONTROL POINTS	5 Levels of Organizational Learning				
			Level 5	Level 4	Level 3	Level 2	Level 1
Strategy	1 Customer focus	1.1 Customer requirements				✔	
		1.2 Customer relationships				✔	
		1.3 Order-to-delivery process				✔	
	2 Leadership	2.1 Business renewal			✔		
		2.2 Focus	✔				
		2.3 Standardization			✔		
		2.4 Adherence	✔				
		2.5 Reflection		✔			
Structure	3 Lean organization	3.1 Team activities				✔	
		3.2 Networked organization				✔	
		3.3 Rewards + recognition				✔	
		3.4 Evaluation + compensation		✔			
		3.5 Lean administration				✔	
	4 Partnering	4.1 Employee value		✔			
		4.2 Comakership			✔		
		4.3 Environmental impact				✔	
		4.4 Social integrity			✔		
	5 Information architecture	5.1 Workplace org. & vis. control		✔			
		5.2 Fast feedback systems				✔	
		5.3 Performance measurement				✔	
		5.4 Kaizen reporting		✔			
Strengths	6 Culture of improvement	6.1 Standardization	✔				
		6.2 Waste-free strategy		✔			
		6.3 Technology diffusion	✔				
		6.4 Education			✔		
	7 Lean production	7.1 Flow production			✔		
		7.2 Multiprocess handling	✔				
		7.3 Leveled, mixed model prod.		✔			
		7.4 Quick changeover		✔			
		7.5 Automation with a human touch	✔				
		7.6 Pull system/coupled production			✔		
		7.7 Production scheduling		✔			
	8 Lean equipment management	8.1 Equip./process improvement		✔			
		8.2 Autonomous maintenance	✔				
		8.3 Planned maintenance			✔		
		8.4 Quality maintenance		✔			
		8.5 Early equipment management	✔				
		8.6 Safety			✔		
		8.7 Equip. invest./maint. prev. design		✔			
	9 Lean engineering	9.1 Design process				✔	
		9.2 Design for QCD				✔	

$\frac{6}{3} = \boxed{2}$

$\frac{20}{5} = \boxed{4}$

$\frac{15}{5} = \boxed{3}$

$\frac{12}{4} = \boxed{3}$

$\frac{12}{4} = \boxed{3}$

$\frac{16}{4} = \boxed{4}$

$\frac{28}{7} = \boxed{4}$

$\frac{28}{7} = \boxed{4}$

$\frac{4}{2} = \boxed{2}$

FIGURE 4-1.
LEAN MANAGEMENT SCOREBOARD

summarizes the Nonesuch company's baseline diagnostic score in the nine keys. The control points also form the basic areas of improvement activities addressed in the annual policy of the strategic improvement cycle (see "Step 3. Define Control Points" in Chapter 5).

In a small, single-plant company, the corporate leadership is generally close enough to the operations level that it can apply the diagnosis directly to that level. Larger organizations with multiple sites may need to apply the diagnosis in stages, with centralized corporate management basing their overall diagnosis on divisional managers' (or even external consultants') assessments of each division. In a large organization, the baseline diagnosis will necessarily be a rough sketch. As management learns the process and gains experience leading improvement cycles, the accuracy of information from the annual diagnosis will increase.

STEP 6. REVIEW STRATEGIC INFORMATION

Armed with knowledge about the company's strong and weak lean management keys, the renewal team next looks at information about its market—customers and competitors—to help it determine which keys are most important to improve in the next five years. The information considered in this step is usually collected as part of traditional strategic planning activities. It is helpful to keep in mind Figure 2-3 (p. 22), which shows how the zero-waste goals of each key contribute to the company's profitability.

Market Position

The renewal team begins this review by assessing the company's market position with the help of a Product/Market Matrix. Figure 4-2 shows the matrix created by the Nonesuch Casting renewal team.

To fill out the Product/Market Matrix, the renewal team identifies all major product types and all customer groups for each segment in which the company competes. These items become the headings for the rows and columns of the matrix. Next the team estimates the annual dollar value of low-end, midrange, and high-end market segments and enters these values in the blanks below the matrix. Finally the team establishes market priorities by applying these three levels to indicate which combinations of product and market segment are most important. For Nonesuch Casting, the analysis shown in Figure 4-2 indicates that small, precision castings are the

Nonesuch Casting Co.

Market / Product Type	Customer 1	Customer 2	Customer 3	Customer 4	Export					
Large castings	L	L	M	M	M					
Medium castings	H	H	H	L	L					
Small, precision castings	H	H	H	L	H					

Market Importance

L = low end $ _____

M = midrange $ _____

H = high end $ _____

Source: Adapted from Kenichi Ohmae, *The Mind of the Strategist* (New York: McGraw-Hill, 1982), p. 44.

FIGURE 4-2.
A NONESUCH PRODUCT/MARKET MATRIX

high-value portion of sales to most of its customers, a priority market in which the *customer focus* and *lean engineering* keys could be important.

Competitor Analysis

Traditional strategic planning in a traditional company has top management compare their company's profitability, market share, pricing, and new products to those of their competitors. In lean developmental planning, these factors are still significant, but it is more important to understand key growth-promoting factors and their relation to future profitability. The lean system distills these growth factors into the nine keys used in the Corporate Diagnosis. Here, they are used to evaluate the competition to highlight areas for development.

The Key Factor Matrix is a tool for comparing the company's and competitors' Corporate Diagnosis scores for important product markets. The results of the company's own Corporate Diagnosis go in the first column.

With the diagnostic criteria fresh in mind, the renewal team then scores each competitor in each key area. Executive teams with a clear understanding of their competitors' markets, processes, advantages, and shortcomings should be able to assign a score without detailed research or special intelligence gathering. Figure 4-3 shows a sample Key Factor Matrix filled in for Nonesuch Casting.

Filling out a Key Factor Matrix for each market in which the company competes will complement its profitability and product/market analysis and sharpen management's understanding of the company's ability to deal with the future.

The Key Factor Matrix in Figure 4-3 highlights strengths and weaknesses of Nonesuch Casting and its competitors and suggests possible development priorities. For example, Nonesuch and its strongest rival, Competitor X, are

Nonesuch Casting Co.

Product: Small, precision castings / Market: Customer 3	You	Your Competitors							
	Nonesuch	Competitor X	Competitor Y	Competitor Z					
1 Customer focus	2	2	3	5					
2 Leadership	4	1	2	4					
3 Lean organization	3	1	2	3					
4 Partnering	3	2	1	3					
5 Information architecture	3	1	2	3					
6 Culture of improvement	4	2	3	5					
7 Lean production	4	1	3	4					
8 Lean equipment management	4	1	2	4					
9 Lean engineering	2	2	3	3					
Total	29	13	21	34					
RELATIVE RANKING									

FIGURE 4-3.
A NONESUCH KEY FACTOR MATRIX

both fairly strong in *customer focus* and *lean engineering,* which parallels the keys identified in relation to the product-market analysis. Note, however, that Nonesuch is relatively weak in *leadership, culture of improvement,* and *lean equipment management,* suggesting that these might be the most important keys to focus on in the initial Development Plan.

STEP 7. DEFINE STRATEGIC KEYS

In light of the results of the Corporate Diagnosis and the company's strategic information, the renewal team looks again at the nine development keys and decides which are most strategically important in helping the company realize its vision over the long term—in this case, the next three to five years. This analysis is assisted by a ranking matrix developed by Yoji Akao (see Figure 4-4). The grid makes it simple to rank the importance of several items by plotting their position in relation to two relevant criteria. As the numbered quadrants suggest, the user first ranks the items in relation to the scale on the vertical axis, then in relation to the horizontal scale. The user then plots the item in the quadrant where these two positions intersect.

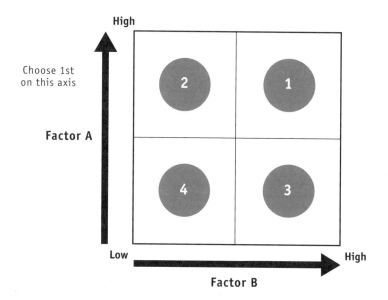

Source: Adapted from Yoji Akao, *Hoshin Kanri* (Portland, Ore.: Productivity Press, 1991), p. 88.

FIGURE 4-4.
RANKING MATRIX

In this case, the renewal team ranks the nine keys according to two factors: first, the *predicted importance* of that key to the target market five years from now, and second, the *current level of excellence* in that key in relation to competitors. Keys that will be the most important to the customer and are also areas of current competitive strength fall in quadrant 1; keys that will also be important but are not currently as strong are in quadrant 2; keys that will not be the most important, but areas in which the company excels are in quadrant 3; and keys that are neither important nor excellent are in quadrant 4. Items in quadrant 1 will be the strongest choices as strategic keys to develop for the long term.

In the Nonesuch case, the renewal team determined that Keys 1 (*customer focus*) and 9 (*lean engineering*) were most important to the customer in the long term, and also the company's strongest competitive areas (see Figure 4-5). The team selected these two keys as its strategic keys for the coming business renewal.

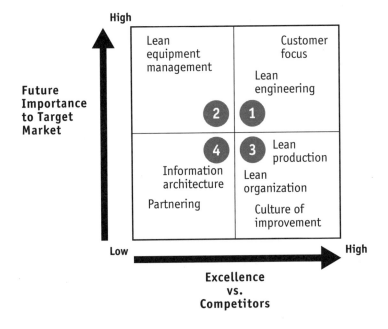

FIGURE 4-5.
NONESUCH RANKING MATRIX FOR CUSTOMER
IMPORTANCE/COMPETITIVE EXCELLENCE MATRIX

STEP 8. PRODUCE A DEVELOPMENT PLAN

The end result of the process in the previous step is the Development Plan. After synthesizing the corporate diagnosis results and other information in Step 7, the renewal team creates a plan that shows the baseline from the Corporate Diagnosis, the strategic keys, and the "big picture" of the sequence for improving all nine keys. This plan is the most important document in the business renewal strategy. Without such a plan, a company cannot fulfill its purpose of building a lean and flexible production system, capable of responding quickly to changes in market conditions.

Figure 4-6 shows Nonesuch Casting's Development Plan for the coming three to five years. The strategic keys are the two areas in which the company plans to reach level 1 by year 5—*customer focus* and *lean engineering*.

The timeframe of a company's Development Plan depends on the relative rates of technological, social, and economic change, which vary from industry to industry. Generally, the Development Plan sets learning and improvement goals in each key for the long term (approximately five years), with a midterm target (three years). These farsighted goals are reached step by step through efforts directed at concrete short-term targets of one year or less. The process of attaining these annual improvement targets is the Strategic Improvement Cycle, addressed in the chapters of Part III.

THE BUSINESS RENEWAL PROCESS

Cornerstones of Growth	Keys to Development	5 Levels of Organizational Learning				
		Level 5	Level 4	Level 3	Level 2	Level 1
		Mass production	System initiation	System development	System maturity	System excellence
Strategy	1 Customer focus				Baseline / Year 3	Year 5
	2 Leadership		Baseline	Year 3	Year 5	
Structure	3 Lean organization			Baseline / Year 3	Year 5	
	4 Partnering			Baseline / Year 3	Year 5	
	5 Information architecture			Baseline / Year 3	Year 5	
Strengths	6 Culture of improvement			Baseline / Year 3	Year 5	
	7 Lean production		Baseline	Year 3	Year 5	
	8 Lean equipment management		Baseline		Year 3 / Year 5	
	9 Lean engineering				Baseline / Year 3	Year 5

FIGURE 4-6.
NONESUCH DEVELOPMENT PLAN

PART III

The Strategic Improvement Cycle

Practice is the best of all instructors.
—Publius Syrus

A SERIOUS DRAWBACK OF TRADITIONAL STRATEGIC PLANNING is that top management planners often do not express their strategy in clear and simple terms to the rest of the organization. As a result, managers and employees may fail to understand the relevance of the plan and their roles in reaching the objectives. The Lean Management System avoids this pitfall through a process that communicates the need for the prescribed changes, describes the changes as concrete targets, clarifies and solicits feedback on the targets, and assures buy-in at all levels for implementing improvement. This process—the "policy bridge" mentioned in Chapter 2—is called the Strategic Improvement Cycle.

The Strategic Improvement Cycle is the mechanism through which the entire company implements the vision and the Development Plan created during top management's business renewal activities. In this cycle, company leaders, acting as a *focus team,* translate the vision and the five-year development plan into a short-term policy that is pursued by everyone in the company in an interactive, cross-functional process. This policy sets out concrete, measurable targets that focus improvement efforts during the next six to twelve months. (For simplicity we will assume an annual cycle throughout Part III.) The midlevel and frontline management become involved in *deployment* and *action teams* to further define the actions needed to meet the targets, then the entire workforce implements these action plans and develops systems for maintaining the new level of performance. Near the end of the improvement cycle, top management conducts another Corporate Diagnosis to observe progress in the various key areas. Then the management team reviews strategic information as it did for business renewal, looks at the diagnosis results and progress in the improvement targets, and reconsiders the policy theme for the next cycle of improvement. After each Business Renewal Process, the company will go through several rounds of the Strategic Improvement Cycle, with the results of each round shaping the policy and targets of the next round.

The process of the Strategic Improvement Cycle is driven by management forms that are used to convey targets and other information from the planning levels of the organization to the implementation level, and reporting forms that tell the planners how the company is progressing toward each target. These forms, shown as examples in the following chapters, are available in blank format from the publisher.

The Business Renewal Process

The Strategic Improvement Cycle

	Phase I: Focus	Phase II: Standardization	Phase III: Adherence	Phase IV: Reflection	Phase I: Focus
Outside Stakeholders	*(hatched)*				
Top Management	*Business Renewal Team* **Vision** 1. Envision the future 2. Analyze the vision 3. Revise the vision 4. Deploy the vision **Development plan** 5. Conduct Corporate Diagnosis 6. Review strategic information 7. Define strategic keys 8. Produce Development Plan	*Focus Team* 1. Organize deployment teams 2. Announce annual policy and transmit Deployment Plans (After deployment teams finish their first two steps:) 3. Play catchball 4. Finalize budgets 5. Summarize	*Focus Team* 1. Complete Plan Summary 2. Conduct Corporate Diagnosis	*Focus Team* 1. Collect information 2. Identify critical performance gaps 3. Identify emergent gaps and barriers 4. Analyze gaps and barriers 5. Summarize	*Focus Team* 1. Select theme and set an overall target 2. Define critical keys 3. Define critical control points 4. Write Proposed Deployment Plans 5. Estimate financial impacts 6. Summarize
	Focus Team 1. Select theme and set an overall target 2. Define critical keys 3. Define critical control points 4. Write proposed deployment plans 5. Estimate financial impacts 6. Summarize	*Deployment Teams* 1. Collect, analyze, evaluate data 2. Determine critical checkpoints 3. Play catchball 4. Write Action Plans	*Deployment Teams* 1. Create a monthly analysis system		
		Action Teams 1. Draw up workcenter plans 2. Assign workteam targets 3. Set personal targets 4. Apply reliable methods	*Action Teams* • Create a visual information system • Maintain a reporting system • Support continuous learning in the workplace		
Middle Management					
Team Leaders and Supervisors					
Operators and Staff					
Documents and Forms	• Vision Statement • Lean Management Scoreboard • Lean Radar Chart • Product/Mrkt. Matrix • Key Factor Matrix • Development Plan — • Target/Means Diagram • X-Type Matrix • Proposed Deployment Plans • Plan Summary (initial)	• Target/Means Diagram • X-Type Matrix • Deployment Plans (confirmed) • Plan Summary (revised) — • Target/Means Diagram • X-Type Matrix • Action Plans — • Planning Sheets • Control Boards • Team Action Plans • Monthly Planner • Daily Planner	• Plan Summary (completed) • Scoreboard • Radar Chart — • Monthly Analysis • Periodic Status Reports — • Control Boards • Daily and Monthly Self-Reports	• Analysis Summary	

FIGURE III-1.

PHASES AND STEPS OF THE LEAN IMPROVEMENT CYCLE

Figure III-1 presents an overview of the phases of the Strategic Improvement Cycle and their relationship to the Business Renewal Process, and lists the documents associated with each phase.

The approach presented in these chapters draws on concepts and tools from hoshin planning and companywide quality deployment developed by Yoji Akao, Ryuji Fukuda, Alberto Galgano, and others.[1]

NOTE

1. See Yoji Akao, *Hoshin Kanri: Policy Deployment for Successful TQM* (1991); Ryuji Fukuda, *Managerial Engineering: Techniques for Improving Quality and Productivity in the Workplace* (1986); Ryuji Fukuda, *CEDAC®: A Tool for Continuous Systematic Improvement* (1990). Policy deployment is explained succinctly in Shoji Shiba, Alan Graham, and David Walden, *A New American TQM: Four Practical Revolutions in Management* (1993), Chapter 14, and in Alberto Galgano, *Companywide Quality Management* (1994), Chapter 18. (All titles are published by Productivity Press, Portland, Oregon.)

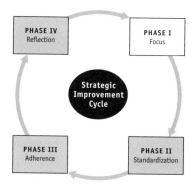

CHAPTER 5

Phase I: Focus

PHASE I OF THE FIRST STRATEGIC IMPROVEMENT CYCLE takes off directly from the vision-building and planning activities of the Business Renewal Cycle. The primary activity of this phase is to convert the development plan into concrete improvement targets for the coming year. During this initial phase of strategic improvement the company determines which keys are critical and assembles an annual improvement policy of concise, measurable targets focusing on those keys.

The activities in this phase are carried out by a *focus team*. In small companies, the focus team may consist of the same people who were on the renewal team that wrote the vision—the CEO, president, and direct reports. In larger companies, however, the focus team activities may be delegated to the top management of individual divisions or plant locations so that deployment and implementation are tailored to the circumstances of each business unit.

The first two phases of the Strategic Improvement Cycle turn the Development Plan into an implementable annual policy. Two documentary tools are employed: the Target/Means Diagram and the X-Type Matrix, both adapted from tools developed by improvement process expert Ryuji Fukuda. The Target/Means Diagram has some elements in common with Fukuda's CEDAC chart, but is used for deployment rather than problem solving. The Target/Means Diagram is a method for articulating a significant

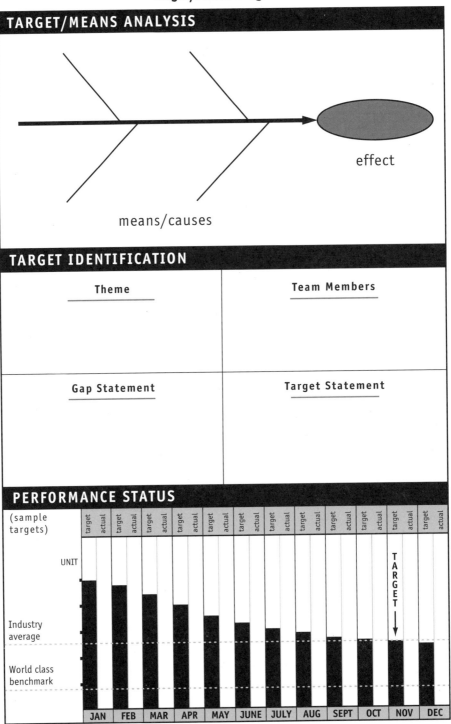

FIGURE 5-1.
BLANK TARGET/MEANS DIAGRAM

performance gap as a problem effect, setting an improvement target, and then determining the causal factors of the problem effect (see Figure 5-1). This method conveniently places a gap statement and a target, causal factors to be explored, and a progress graph onto one document, usually produced as a large wall chart to share the information visually.

The Target/Means Diagram is a good way to involve a group of people in improvement activities since it makes all relevant information available at a glance. Moreover, it facilitates successive levels of problem solving within the same organization. During the Strategic Improvement Cycle the diagram is used at several levels as a means to break down the overall target effect—the annual improvement target for a particular theme—into successively more manageable targets, culminating in Action Plans carried out by teams across the entire organization.

The X-Type Matrix (see Figure 5-2) is a useful cross-functional document that summarizes the means and target measures developed through the Target/Means Diagrams; it is the embodiment of the annual policy. The management team fills it in clockwise, entering data on the blank lines along each side; the blackened squares in the shaded corners indicate the connection between the data on either side. In the Focus phase, the top management team uses the X-Type Matrix to record the keys selected as critical for a particular annual theme, critical control points to track for each critical key, specific targets for each critical control point, and the cost savings or revenue anticipated from meeting each target. The matrix also records the ownership of each improvement goal. In Phase I, the members of the top management focus team are responsible for carrying forward the specific Proposed Deployment Plans. Phase II of strategic improvement will use an even more specific X-Type Matrix to further develop the policy at the deployment team (departmental) level and the action team (workcenter) level.

The focus team develops the annual policy through a six-step process:

1. Select a theme and set an overall target
2. Define critical keys
3. Define control points
4. Write action plans
5. Finalize profit plans and prepare detailed budgets
6. Summarize

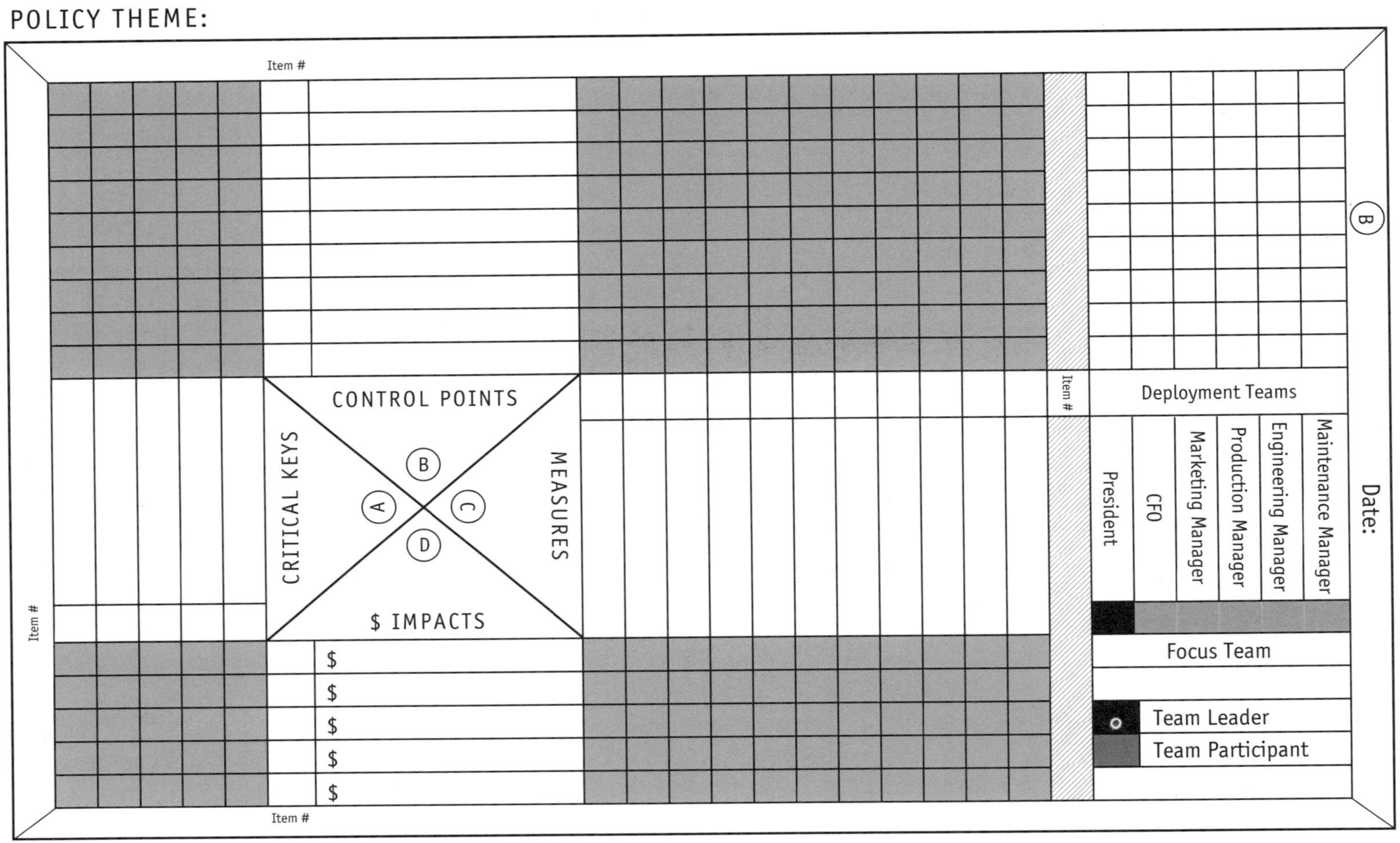

POLICY THEME:

Date:

(B)

Deployment Teams

Maintenance Manager
Engineering Manager
Production Manager
Marketing Manager
CFO
President

Focus Team
Team Leader
Team Participant

Item #

MEASURES

CONTROL POINTS

(B) (C) (D) (A)

CRITICAL KEYS

$ IMPACTS

$
$
$
$
$

Item #

Item #

Item #

FIGURE 5-2.
BLANK X-TYPE MATRIX

STEP 1. SELECT AN IMPROVEMENT THEME AND SET AN OVERALL TARGET

Selecting the Theme

To transform the company vision and development plan into a context for daily activity, the focus team must first develop an annual improvement theme. This theme will help establish a clear direction and unifying tone for the firm's short-term improvement activities. The right theme leverages the company's limited resources by focusing everyone's attention on a defined set of problems. A good theme can guide all improvement programs, including plans prescribed for project teams as well as voluntary activities in quality circles and employee suggestion programs.

The focus team may generate many ideas for an overall improvement theme. The team should select no more than three themes for each improvement cycle. Since each theme must be deployed separately and the targets for each theme multiply exponentially from level to level, choosing a large number of themes can create a managerial nightmare. If the team chooses more than one theme, it is usually because the themes are very closely related (overlapping topics), or are very different (equally significant topics that cannot be put off). In the Nonesuch example, the focus team chooses a single theme, which is not an unusual practice.

To find an annual theme, it is often useful to think about what actions are needed to increase short-term profits. Profit is influenced by a number of variables, each of which could serve as an improvement theme; the following formula—a variation on the one presented in Chapter 1—illustrates their interrelation:

$$\prod = Q \bullet (P[q,s] - C[q,s])$$

where $\prod$ = profit

   Q = quantity of product sold

   P = sales price

   C = unit cost

   q = quality

   s = speed

   $P[q,s]$ = price as a function of quality and speed

   $C[q,s]$ = cost as a function of quality and speed

Price is a positive function of both quality and speed; this means that the better the quality or the faster a product can be produced or brought to market, the higher the price its producer may charge. Under lean production conditions, cost is a negative function of quality and speed; that is, the better the quality or the faster a product can be produced, the lower the cost. This is a major difference between lean production and mass production, where the opposite assumptions about the link between cost and quality hold.

The elements of this equation can be used to form several possible themes for improvement. Here is a short list of themes generated by Nonesuch Casting Company's focus team:

- Increase market share
- Improve cost control
- Improve total quality
- Improve cycle time

We can easily understand these themes and their effect on profit by relating them to the elements of the equation. For example, raising productivity will help the company increase profitability by increasing Q, quantity, and perhaps by decreasing C, cost. Improving cost control will increase profitability by decreasing C, cost. Increasing market share will increase profitability by increasing Q, quantity. Improving total quality or cycle time will increase profitability by permitting the company to increase P, price, and/or decrease C, cost.

Once the team has generated a list of candidates for the annual improvement theme, it prioritizes them by ranking the importance of the corresponding elements of the profit equation. Yoji Akao's ranking matrix (introduced in Chapter 4 in relation to selection of strategic keys) is useful for sorting out these elements.

After the focus team makes a list of possible improvement themes, they rank each one according to two factors: urgency and achievability. Themes that are urgent and not too difficult to achieve fall into quadrant 1; urgent themes that are more difficult to achieve are in quadrant 2; and so on. The themes in quadrant 1 are the best candidates for the company's annual theme.

Figure 5-3 shows Nonesuch Casting's urgency/achievability analysis, which ranks the four elements as follows:

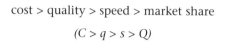

cost > quality > speed > market share

$(C > q > s > Q)$

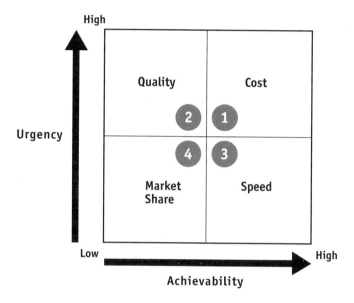

FIGURE 5-3.
RANKING MATRIX FOR SELECTING THE THEME
(URGENCY/ACHIEVABILITY)

The most urgent and achievable short-term profit opportunity for Nonesuch lay in the reduction of its manufacturing costs. The parent company, Nonesuch Automobile Corporation, expected substantial price reductions in the coming year, even for the more costly precision castings, so cost reduction was critical. Quality was ranked next important for improvement, because of Nonesuch Casting's chronic quality problems. Speed, although important, was ranked behind quality, again because Nonesuch's primary customer, its parent company, insisted on perfect quality before all else. Market share was ranked last, because Nonesuch reasoned that if it reduced cost and therefore price, market share would naturally increase. As a result of this simple exercise, the Nonesuch focus team decided that cost reduction should be the basis of the annual theme, and came up with the following theme statement:

> Cost Down, Competitiveness Up!

Defining a Target

After choosing an annual theme, the focus team sets a specific annual target to achieve. To determine a target, the team first analyzes the main theme-related challenge facing the company in the coming year and articulates that in the form of a "gap statement." A gap statement briefly describes the company's current status in the theme area and how that varies from world class measures and the expectations of external and internal customers. It is used again in Step 2 to pinpoint deficient performance in each critical key.

The purpose of a gap statement is twofold. First, the act of writing a gap statement requires a consensus on the deficiencies in each profit factor (and later in each critical key). Developing the gap statement often instills a spirit of solidarity among its creators. Second, the gap statement is a snapshot of the company's condition at a specified point in time and is the baseline from which improvement will be measured. The annual policy gap statement will form part of the company's basic improvement consciousness, helping employees throughout the organization perceive opportunities. The gap statement for Nonesuch Casting Company was:

> In 1995, Nonesuch Casting's cost (including delivery) was $2.50/unit, nearly 20% higher than the world class benchmark of $2.10/unit. As a result, Nonesuch has difficulty competing in precision castings.

The target for the company is a performance measure that will narrow the gap. The Nonesuch focus team set the following improvement target:

> Nonesuch will reduce its production and delivery costs to $2.25/unit by Nov. 15, 1996.

Nonesuch Casting Co.   **Theme Target/Means Diagram**

TARGET/MEANS ANALYSIS

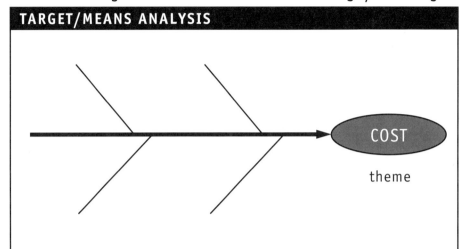

TARGET IDENTIFICATION

Theme	Focus Team
Cost Down, Competitiveness Up!	President Production Manager CFO Engineering Manager Marketing Manager Maintenance Manager

Gap Statement	Target Statement
In 1995, Nonesuch's cost (including delivery) was $2.50/unit, nearly 20% higher than the world class benchmark of $2.10/unit. As a result, Nonesuch has difficulty competing in precision castings.	Nonesuch will reduce its production and delivery costs to $2.25/unit by Nov. 15, 1996.

PERFORMANCE STATUS

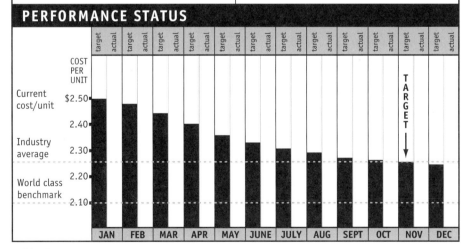

FIGURE 5-4.
TARGET/MEANS DIAGRAM FOR ANNUAL POLICY

The focus team expresses the gap statement and the target for the annual policy on a Target/Means Diagram. As its name indicates, this document also guides the development of the means of achieving the target, and tracks progress against monthly targets along the way. Figure 5-4 shows the Target/Means Diagram developed by the Nonesuch Casting focus team at this point. The theme, gap statement, and target appear in the middle portion, along with the names of focus team members. The bottom part of the diagram charts interim monthly cost targets toward the annual target and makes the gap visual through horizontal dashed lines showing the world class and industry levels for cost. The fishbone diagram at the top will be used in Step 2.

STEP 2. DEFINE CRITICAL KEYS AND TARGETS FOR EACH

At the end of the Business Renewal Process, the top management team laid out a Development Plan that identified strategic keys in which the company plans to excel in the next five years. In defining annual policy, the focus team reviews the Development Plan to determine the keys that are critical to upgrade in the short term to promote the medium- and long-term goals. These critical keys will later be broken into critical control points for action and improvement toward the annual policy target.

In some cases the critical keys will be the same as the strategic keys set out in the Development Plan. The nine keys are interrelated, however, and excellence in any single key generally requires adequate development in others. Often, other keys may need to be advanced in the short term to support the strategic keys in which the company hopes to excel in the future. Without the groundwork in these other critical keys, efforts in the strategic key will get nowhere. *Culture of improvement* is a good example of a key many companies need to upgrade to support other, strategic keys; companies must address old blame and coverup behaviors before they can ever hope to progress in lean production or equipment management.

Determining the critical keys for each Strategic Improvement Cycle is a process that requires some real thought. The focus team views each strategic key in the development plan as a distinct target, then considers what is required to reach each of these targets. The team looks for imbalances in the company's previous development, trying to identify keys in which the company lags behind.

In any given policy cycle, the company should limit its focus to two or three critical keys. If analysis of the development plan fails to yield clear selections, then the focus team can again use a ranking matrix to narrow the choice. This time the team considers the relationship between each key's *effectiveness*—how well it gets the job done—and its *efficiency*—how long it takes and how much it costs. Because the annual target has been chosen primarily on the basis of necessity, the team should be most concerned about the effectiveness of a key toward achieving the target, and secondarily consider which of the effective keys gives the best return on the investment. We use the Nonesuch Casting example to demonstrate how to carry out this analysis.

When the Nonesuch focus team analyzed their Development Plan (Figure 4-6) and competitor benchmarking (Figure 4-3), they recognized that the company lagged behind in Keys 2 and 8, *leadership* and *lean equipment management,* and also saw their keys 1, 5, and 9 (*customer focus, information architecture,* and *lean engineering*)—as potentially critical. To develop the list of critical keys to address in the first year, they applied the effectiveness/efficiency ranking analysis and came up with the diagram shown in Figure 5-5. Their entries in this diagram are explained as follows.

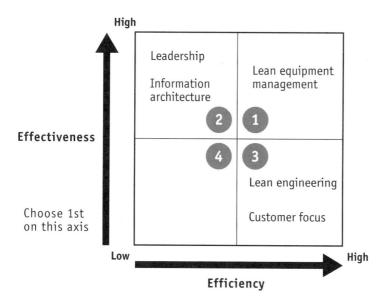

FIGURE 5-5.
RANKING MATRIX FOR SELECTING CRITICAL KEYS
(EFFECTIVENESS/EFFICIENCY)

Referring to the Development Plan, the Nonesuch focus team reasoned that the company was already relatively well developed in the areas of *customer focus* and *lean engineering*. As the diagram shows, the team felt that working on these two keys, though they would be relatively efficient to implement, was not the most effective approach for the desired result—cost reduction. To improve cost, a different approach was needed in the short run. Of the remaining three keys, Key 8, *lean equipment management,* seemed the most effective. *Lean equipment management* directly reduces cost by increasing equipment availability and efficiency and improving quality. This key was also considered the most efficient means of reducing cost, because the major cost of implementing it is intensive training, which is known to give an exceptional return on investment. Keys 2 and 5, *leadership* and *information architecture,* were thought effective but less efficient means of achieving cost reduction because although they are necessary to implement *lean equipment management,* they affect cost only indirectly.

Reading from the effectiveness/efficiency matrix, the focus team ranked the five keys as follows:

$$\text{lean equipment management} > \text{leadership} = \text{information architecture} > \text{lean engineering} = \text{customer focus}$$

The Nonesuch focus team reviewed the ranking and recognized that three keys would be too much to take on, so they limited the choice to two. Recognizing that several aspects of *information architecture* would actually be supported by effective improvements in the other two top-ranked keys, the team selected *lean equipment management* and *leadership* as the critical keys for the first year's policy.

Once the priorities are established, the team adds these critical keys to the fishbone diagram at the top of the Target/Means Diagram. Figure 5-6 shows this on the Nonesuch focus team's diagram. This indicates that the critical keys are the primary means for reaching the target effect shown in the oval—cost.

The focus team then begins an X-Type Matrix for the annual policy by filling in the critical keys in the designated section on the left side. Item numbers are assigned so that related information can be tracked as the chart is read. In our system, we use numbers that correlate with the sequence of

Nonesuch Casting Co.   **Theme Target/Means Diagram**

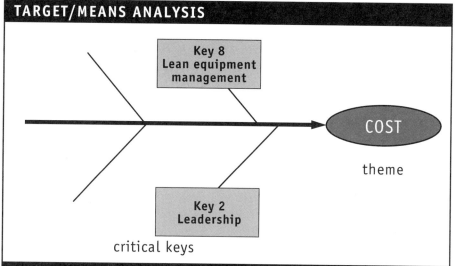

TARGET/MEANS ANALYSIS

TARGET IDENTIFICATION

Theme	Focus Team	
Cost Down, Competitiveness Up!	President CFO Marketing Manager	Production Manager Engineering Manager Maintenance Manager

Gap Statement	Target Statement
In 1995, Nonesuch's cost (including delivery) was $2.50/unit, nearly 20% higher than the world class benchmark of $2.10/unit. As a result, Nonesuch has difficulty competing in precision castings.	Nonesuch will reduce its production and delivery costs to $2.25/unit by Nov. 15, 1996.

PERFORMANCE STATUS

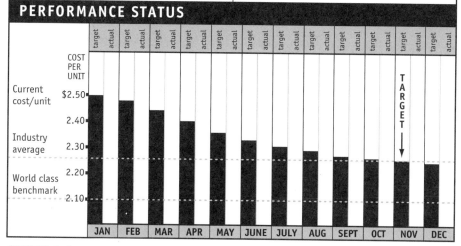

FIGURE 5-6.
TARGET/MEANS DIAGRAM SHOWING THE CRITICAL KEYS

the nine keys and their control points from the system developed in the *Corporate Diagnosis* book. Figure 5-7 shows the Nonesuch critical keys entered on an Annual Policy X-Type Matrix (see section A). This matrix will be filled in section by section in the remaining steps of the Focus phase.

Next, the focus team draws up a separate Target/Means Diagram for each critical key. Figure 5-8 depicts the Nonesuch Target/Means Diagram for its most critical key, lean equipment management. Note that the key is stated as the "effect" of the fishbone chart. The factors that contribute to the target in that effect—the critical control points—will be determined in Step 3.

As the gap statement indicates, the Nonesuch focus team used overall equipment effectiveness (OEE, the product of equipment availability, performance, and quality rates) as the measure for the lean equipment management key. The team set a target to reach 70 percent OEE within a year. The target graph indicates that the company must eventually achieve an 85 percent OEE to be world class.

STEP 3. DETERMINE CRITICAL CONTROL POINTS

In the Target/Means Diagram for Step 2 (Figure 5-8), the critical keys were the means of reaching the overall annual target for cost reduction. In Step 3 the team gets even more specific and treats each critical key as a target for which other, more detailed means will be determined. These means—the critical control points—will form the basis of specific action plans in Step 4.

As Chapter 4 mentioned, the control points are the specific areas in which learning and improvement are measured in each key; the control points for each key appear on the Lean Management Scoreboard in Figure 4-1 (page 51). These are the areas in which a company is audited during the Corporate Diagnosis (see Chapter 4) and consequently are the areas in which improvement is charted on the Target/Means Diagram for each critical key. Just as some keys are more critical for short-term improvement, some control points will also be more effective in achieving the annual policy target.

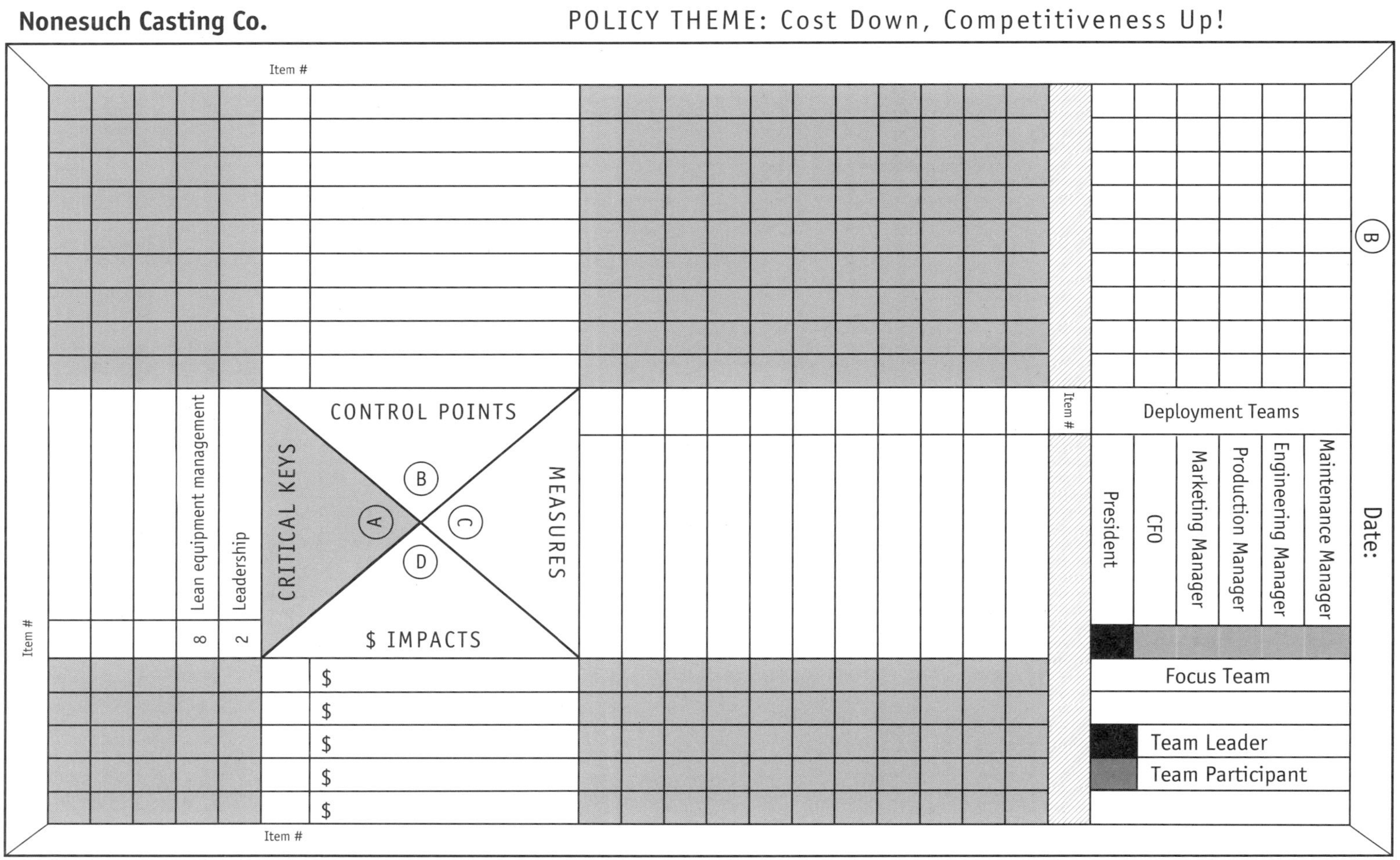

Nonesuch Casting Co.

POLICY THEME: Cost Down, Competitiveness Up!

(B)

Date:

Deployment Teams

Maintenance Manager
Engineering Manager
Production Manager
Marketing Manager
CFO
President

Focus Team
Team Leader
Team Participant

Item #

MEASURES

CONTROL POINTS

(C)

(B)   (D)

(A)

$ IMPACTS

CRITICAL KEYS

$
$
$
$
$

Item #

Leadership	2		
Lean equipment management	8		

Item #

FIGURE 5-7
ANNUAL POLICY X-TYPE MATRIX SHOWING THE CRITICAL KEYS

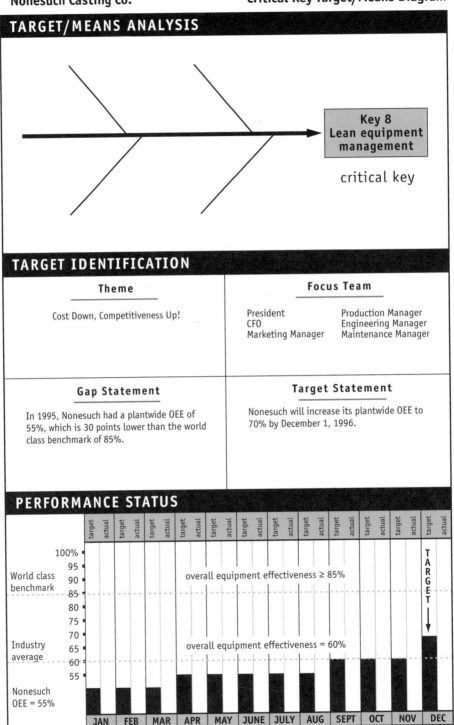

FIGURE 5-8.
TARGET/MEANS DIAGRAM FOR THE LEAN EQUIPMENT
MANAGEMENT CRITICAL KEY

The focus team begins its analysis of critical control points by listing the control points for each critical key. For example, the Nonesuch team would start with Key 8, *lean equipment management:*

Control point 1   *Equipment/process improvement*

Control point 2   *Autonomous maintenance*

Control point 3   *Planned maintenance*

Control point 4   *Quality maintenance*

Control point 5   *Early equipment management*

Control point 6   *Safety*

Control point 7   *Equipment investment/maintenance prevention design*

From such a list, the focus team again applies effectiveness/efficiency ranking analysis to narrow the choice. The team should select no more than four of the control points as critical; proceeding with more than four quickly becomes unwieldy. Figure 5-9 shows the Nonesuch team's matrix.

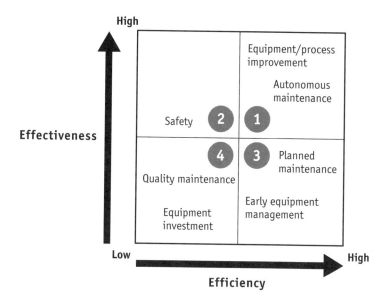

FIGURE 5-9.
RANKING MATRIX FOR SELECTING CRITICAL CONTROL POINTS
(EFFECTIVENESS/EFFICIENCY)

In the Nonesuch Casting example, the focus team ranked *equipment/process improvement* and *autonomous maintenance* above all others in effectiveness and efficiency. The team also ranked safety as a highly effective control point. The team felt that attention in these three areas would reinforce improvements in *information architecture,* a key they had almost selected as a critical key.

The focus team enters the critical control points as labels on the fishbone at the top of the Target/Means Diagram (see Figure 5-10 for the completed Nonesuch diagram). In the next step, each critical control point will be translated into a Deployment Plan.

To ensure good cross-functional communication and coordination, the focus team adds the critical control points in section B of the Annual Policy X-Type Matrix (see Figure 5-11). Note how the shading in the corner sections is used to indicate which control points belong to which key. Using the outside corner of the matrix (also labeled "B"), the team also indicates which individuals (in this case members of the top management focus team) and/or organizational units will own and take responsibility for each control point.

STEP 4. WRITE PROPOSED DEPLOYMENT PLANS

The previous step assigned responsibility for each control point. In Step 4, members of the focus team prepare Proposed Deployment Plans for their areas of responsibility. These plans are called "proposed" because they are subject to revision by the Deployment Teams through a process called *catchball,* described in detail in Chapter 6. The confirmed Deployment Plans will follow the same format.

The Deployment Plan is like a Target/Means Diagram in which the critical control points—the means in the previous step—now become the target for further analysis. The manager in charge of the control point enters the theme, owners, and other information at the top, then develops gap and target statements for the control point, along with a performance graph to chart progress toward the target measure. Instead of specifying the means for each control point target in a fishbone diagram, however, the manager suggests project approaches that could help attain the target. The manager describes general projects rather than dictating specific improvement ideas

Nonesuch Casting Co.   **Critical Key Target/Means Diagram**

TARGET/MEANS ANALYSIS

| Autonomous maintenance | Equipment/ process improvement |

→ **Key 8 Lean equipment management**

critical key

Safety

critical control points

TARGET IDENTIFICATION

Theme

Cost Down, Competitiveness Up!

Focus Team

President   Production Manager
CFO   Engineering Manager
Marketing Manager   Maintenance Manager

Gap Statement

In 1995, Nonesuch had a plantwide OEE of 55%, which is 30 points lower than the world class benchmark of 85%.

Target Statement

Nonesuch will increase its plantwide OEE to 70% by December 1, 1996.

PERFORMANCE STATUS

World class benchmark

overall equipment effectiveness ≥ 85%

Industry average

overall equipment effectiveness = 60%

Nonesuch OEE < 55%

100% 95 90 85 80 75 70 65 60 55

TARGET ↓

JAN FEB MAR APR MAY JUNE JULY AUG SEPT OCT NOV DEC

FIGURE 5-10.
TARGET/MEANS DIAGRAM FOR THE LEAN EQUIPMENT MANAGE-MENT CRITICAL KEY SHOWING CRITICAL CONTROL POINTS

Nonesuch Casting Co.

POLICY THEME: Cost Down, Competitiveness Up!

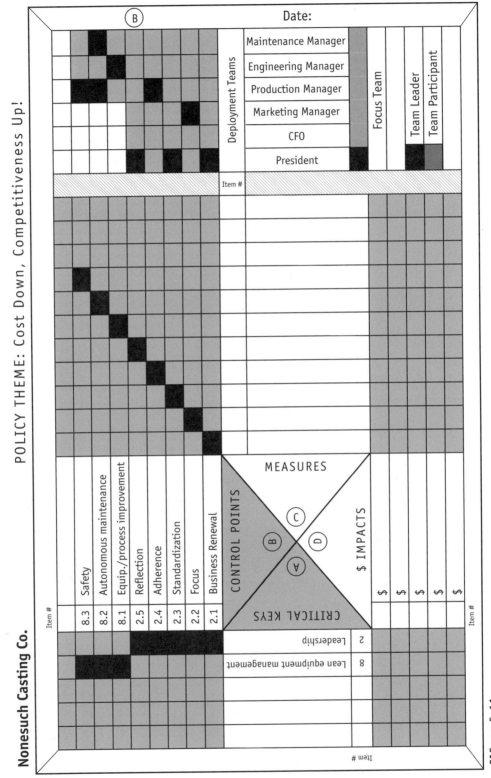

Figure 5-11.
ANNUAL POLICY X-TYPE MATRIX SHOWING CRITICAL CONTROL POINTS AND RESPONSIBILITIES

for two reasons. Implementation plans that are too detailed tend to discourage employee involvement and dampen enthusiasm. Moreover, the Lean Management System shapes the specific decisions and details of improvement projects through a process of policy deployment and daily work. This approach is described step by step in Chapters 6, 7, and 8.

Figure 5-12 shows a Nonesuch Casting Proposed Deployment Plan for the equipment/process improvement control point, which is owned by the engineering manager. (This control point happens to be so closely linked with its key, *lean equipment management,* that the gap, target, and performance graph track the same measure—overall equipment effectiveness [OEE]. Other *lean equipment management* control points will have different measures of success that ultimately will also contribute to improvement in OEE.)

When the Proposed Deployment Plans are completed, the focus team enters the target measures in section C of the Annual Policy X-Type Matrix (below the names of the team members); Figure 5-13 shows Nonesuch Casting's matrix. Again, it uses shading in the corner sections to link the measures to the pertinent control points.

STEP 5. ESTIMATE FINANCIAL IMPACTS

The focus team next needs to consider the financial impact of improvement. For each critical control point, the team conducts an in-depth analysis to determine how much money the company will make or save by improving it. The team then enters these figures in section D of the Annual Policy X-Type Matrix (see the $ Impacts section of Figure 5-13). In the figure, for example, the company projects saving $2 million as a result of improving OEE, since increasing equipment effectiveness will make it unnecessary to purchase a new machine.

In some cases, financial impacts may be set as a policy matter: the company *must* save a certain amount. The team must then reconcile estimated impacts of the control points with critical key financial targets. If the control point financial impact estimates do not tally with the target for the critical key, the team may look for additional means to reach the critical key targets.

Deployment Plan

Nonesuch Casting Co.
Key: Lean equipment management
Control Point: Equipment/process improvement
Item #: 8.1
Item Owner: Engineering Manager
Unit: Lean Equipment Management Initiative

Theme: Cost Down, Competition Up!

Date Updated:
Next Review:
Review Team:

Gap Statement

During the past year, Nonesuch has demonstrated an estimated plantwide OEE of 55%, which is 30 percentage points below the world class benchmark of 85%; and as a result, Nonesuch production costs have been at least $.25.unit higher than they should be.

Target Statement

Nonesuch will increase its plantwide OEE to 70% by December 31, 1996.

Core Objectives

The core objective of *equipment/process improvement* is to raise overall equipment effectiveness (OEE), through cross-functional teamwork involving maintenance, engineering, and production.

$OEE = A \times P \times Q$

A = Availability Rate
P = Performance Rate
Q = Rate of Quality

Suggested Strategies

The company will adopt a classic TPM implementation strategy, as recommended by the Japan Institute of Plant Maintenance program.

The engineering manager will be certified in TPM in Japan by the JIPM. Upon his return he will develop a program suited to the production environment of Nonesuch Casting.

Shopfloor champions for TPM implementation will be chosen. Two or more may also be sent to Japan for JIPM certification. The Production Coordinator and Team Leader 1 are good candidates.

It is anticipated that the company will adopt a model line program to pioneer TPM practices in a small area. The first model machine will be the 800-ton press, where Team Leader 1 works.

Performance Status

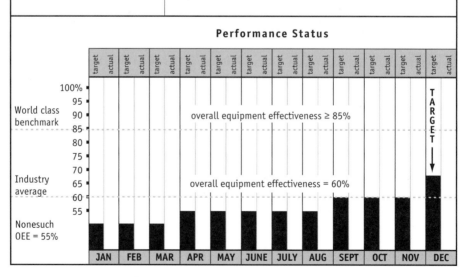

FIGURE 5-12.
PROPOSED DEPLOYMENT PLAN FOR A CRITICAL CONTROL POINT

Nonesuch Casting Co.

POLICY THEME: Cost Down, Competitiveness Up!

Ⓑ

Date:

	Deployment Teams						Focus Team	Team Leader	Team Participant
Item #	Maintenance Manager	Engineering Manager	Production Manager	Marketing Manager	CFO	President			

Item #								
8.3						Reduce lost time accidents by 50% by Dec. 31, 1996.
8.2						Carry out initial cleanings by May 1, 1996.
8.1						Raise OEE to 70% by Dec. 1, 1996.
2.5						Complete Analysis Sheets and Summary by Dec. 1, 1996.
2.4						Conduct Corporate Diagnosis by Nov. 1, 1996.
2.3						Confirm Plan Summary by Feb. 1, 1996.
2.2						Establish Annual Policy by Jan. 1, 1996.
2.1						Finish Business Renewal Cycle by Dec. 1, 1995.

MEASURES

CONTROL POINTS

Ⓒ

Ⓑ   Ⓓ

Ⓐ

CRITICAL KEYS

$ IMPACTS

Item #		
8.3	Safety	
8.2	Autonomous maintenance	
8.1	Equip./process improvement	
2.5	Reflection	
2.4	Adherence	
2.3	Standardization	
2.2	Focus	
2.1	Business Renewal	

		Item #	$ IMPACTS
Leadership	2	2	$ ———
Lean equipment management	8	8.1	$2 million
		8.2	$ (negative)
		8.3	$10,000
			$

FIGURE 5-13.
ANNUAL POLICY X-TYPE MATRIX SHOWING CONTROL POINT TARGET MEASURES (c) AND FINANCIAL IMPACTS (D)

STEP 6. SUMMARIZE

To summarize its annual policy, the focus team completes an Initial Plan Summary document; the one for Nonesuch Casting is pictured in Figure 5-14. The team enters each critical key and corresponding control points, assigning reference numbers based on the entries on the completed X-Type Matrix. The Initial Plan Summary indicates the owner of each item, and the basic strategy proposed and target set for each. The team also projects when it expects action to begin.

The summary document contains space to record actual completion dates and actual levels of each performance measure. This record will be useful during the Adherence phase as a simple way to identify targets that have not been met. This Initial Plan Summary becomes the company's official Plan Summary after revisions and the addition of specific checkpoint targets set by midlevel managers and other members of the deployment teams. This process is described in Chapter 6.

Nonesuch Casting Co.

Plan Summary (Initial)

Date:

Critical Keys	Control Points	Item #	Owner	Strategy	Target	Actual	Start	Complete	Notes
Leadership									
	Business Renewal	2	President	Lean Mgt. System	Done by:				
		2.1	"	Development Plan	12/1/95				
	Focus	2.2	Marketing manager	Annual Policy	1/1/96				
	Standardization	2.3	President	Action Plan	2/1/96				
	Adherence	2.4a	Production manager	Self-Reports	3/1/96				
		2.4b	"	Corporate Diagnosis	11/11/96				
	Reflection	2.5	President	Analysis summary	12/1/96				
Lean equipment management		8	Engineering manager	Model equipment	OEE = 70%				
	Equip./process impr.	8.1	Engineering manager	Model equipment	OEE = 70%				
	Autonomous maint.	8.2	Production manager	1st 3 steps of AM	IC by 6/1/96				
	Safety	8.3	Production manager	DuPont program	LTA down 50%				

FIGURE 5-14.
INITIAL PLAN SUMMARY

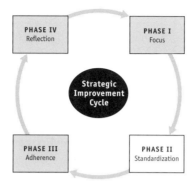

CHAPTER 6

Phase II: Standardization

A MAJOR SHORTCOMING OF TRADITIONAL strategic planning is that top management's plans often have little connection to the daily work of the rest of the company. Production workers and office staff—the people who actually add value to products and services—go about their activities as usual. As a result, even the best plans produce little significant change. In contrast, the Lean Management System realizes the company vision by instilling the attitude of Delta Zero in every employee and building the company's annual policy (developed in Phase I) into daily work—in effect deploying and implementing the policy into a standard operating procedure.

Standardization, Phase II of the Strategic Improvement Cycle, is the process through which the annual policy is deployed into the organization. We call it "Standardization" because these activities are meant to create alignment toward a set of linked goals, at whatever level the goals are managed. Just as people synchronize their watches before parting with the aim of getting back together at a certain time, the Standardization phase synchronizes improvement plans at various levels with the aim of meeting certain shared targets. Through Standardization activities, the departments, teams, and individuals clearly understand their specific roles in attaining the overall company vision and then carry them out methodically. During this phase, the company establishes one of the most important features of lean management—a body of informed, aligned workers whose creativity and process expertise are acknowledged by management and, more important, keenly felt within themselves. Leaders of world class companies who wish to standardize their policies for change take great care to involve their employees and actively listen to the information they can share.

The translation of annual policy into precise reference points and critical measures—the tools to help deliver the year's improvement activities—naturally requires a great deal of employee involvement. Whereas activity in the Focus phase was limited to top management, the Standardization phase consists of activities to transmit information throughout the company—upward and horizontally, as well as downward. The circle of participants now includes not just top management, but middle management, supervisors, and frontline employees, working together in deployment and action teams that overlap management levels and traditional functional divisions. The top management focus team provides a strategy for deployment; the deployment team finalizes action plans; and the action teams implement these plans. The number of deployment and action teams will depend on the size, structure, and maturity of the company.

THE PROCESS OF STANDARDIZATION

Standardization activities take place in three subphases: organization, policy deployment, and implementation. Top management—the focus team—begins by organizing the deployment teams that will carry forward the annual policy. Each team includes a top management representative—one of the people from the focus team. In addition, it includes middle managers (and sometimes frontline team leaders or supervisors) who have a stake in particular critical keys and control points listed on the Annual Policy X-Type Matrix from the previous phase. Since the keys and control points bridge several traditional functional areas, deployment team membership is likely to be cross-functional rather than drawn from a single department.

In the deployment subphase, the focus team passes the Proposed Deployment Plans developed in Phase I to the deployment teams, initiating a feedback process called *catchball*.[1] Catchball is a reality check based on specific knowledge that resides in various parts of the organization, and specifically, closer to the operating level. The purpose of catchball is to create alignment with the annual policy by affirming top management's Deployment Plans at the middle management and support levels before moving forward—and if necessary adjusting the plans so that they can be affirmed. If a deployment team's analysis shows that the plans or targets tossed its way won't work for some reason, it tosses them back to the focus team with recommended changes. Similarly, deployment teams play catchball between each other and with functional management to secure any necessary outside support they need to achieve the requested target. Figure 6-1 depicts some of these vertical and horizontal exchanges. Catchball works on the premise that any plan arising from dialogue between the parties involved will be stronger than a plan simply handed down without discussion. Although this process requires a little time, the result is a set of Deployment Plans that managers and staff have committed to implementing.

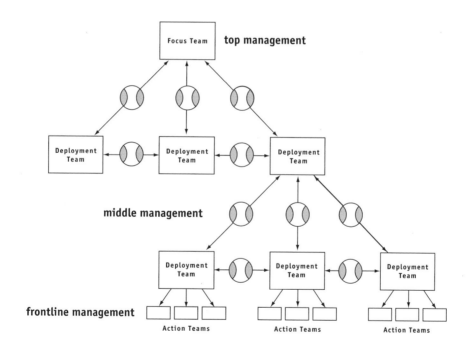

Source: Adapted from Shoji Shiba, Alan Graham, and David Walden, *A New American TQM: Four Practical Revolutions in Management* (Portland, Ore.: Productivity Press, 1993), p. 434.

FIGURE 6-1.
CATCHBALL IN THE LEAN MANAGEMENT SYSTEM

After the Deployment Plans are affirmed, the members of the deployment teams carry them forward for implementation through action teams. Action team membership includes middle management, supervisors, frontline employees, and support staff. The action teams set increasingly specific plans and targets for workcenters, workteams, and individual employees, then oversee the implementation of improvements, using "reliable methods"—systematic improvement approaches that are known to produce results. Just-in-time, total productive maintenance, total quality management, CEDAC (cause-and-effect diagram with the addition of cards), and concurrent engineering are major reliable methods that are frequently applied. Figure III-1 (p. 62) gives an overview of team activities in Phase II.

FOCUS TEAM ACTIVITIES

The top management focus team has five basic activities in Phase II:

1. Organize deployment teams
2. Announce annual policy and transmit Deployment Plans
3. Play catchball
4. Finalize budgets
5. Summarize

The process is described in the following sections for a relatively flat company with top, middle, and frontline supervisory levels of management. In companies with more than these three management levels, the five-step process may be repeated from level to level until the desired degree of deployment is achieved.

Step 1. Organize Deployment Teams

Successful implementation of the annual policy depends on confirmation of the Deployment Plans by the teams who will ultimately have to manage their implementation. The focus team's first task is to determine what deployment teams need to be formed and who should participate on them. There should be at least one team for each critical key; the critical control points selected for each key may be best deployed by several teams with varying makeup. The deployment team for *leadership*—not a critical key but included to track planning and deployment—consists of the focus team plus any necessary additional support. Teams are sometimes based on functional lines, but it may be important to develop new cross-functional teams (such as high-level design teams or business process reengineering teams) to lead specific initiatives related to emerging needs. The important thing is to charter teams that relate to the critical keys and control points identified in Phase I, and to fill them with the people best positioned to promote both strategic cross-functional communication and focused improvement in daily work.

In addition to one representative (or more) from the top management focus team, each deployment team may include plant and department managers and their staffs as well as team members from improvement and product development teams. These teams typically consist of employees above the supervisory level, although supervisors are sometimes included in teams formed within individual plants, especially if the organization is very flat. The Nonesuch Company was relatively small; it had one deployment team for the *lean equipment management* key for the entire plant—a cross-functional Lean Equipment Management Initiative (LEMI) Team, which included the engineering, production, and maintenance managers from the focus team, production and toolroom coordinators, and a maintenance technician.

Step 2. Announce Annual Policy and Transmit Deployment Plans

To kick off the policy deployment process, the chief executive officer presents the annual policy to the entire company, describing its overall improvement theme and critical keys, and naming the deployment teams that will be formed. In some companies, the overall improvement target will be confidential information that is not appropriate to publicize. As much as possible, however, management should keep all employees aware of the company's financial condition and its strategic challenges.

After the CEO's presentation, the focus team transmits to each deployment team a Proposed Deployment Plan for each control point assigned to that team. This document provides enough information for each deployment team to set up its own Target/Means Diagrams and to track cross-functional relationships that affect implementation.

Step 3. Play Catchball with Deployment Teams

After the CEO's kickoff, the deployment teams meet, do further analysis, and determine critical checkpoints—another finer level of means analysis related to the focus team's critical control points as targets. (These activities are described later in the chapter in the context of deployment team activities. At this point it may be useful to preview those sections.) Then each deployment team meets with the top management team to discuss what does and doesn't work in the proposed Deployment Plans and targets. This discussion between teams is the catchball process described at the beginning of the chapter.

Catchball takes place at all levels, both vertically (top down and bottom up) and horizontally (between deployment teams and departments that have a stake in implementation plans). However, catchball is not a negotiation of conflicting ideas and desires; rather, it is a reconciliation of a proposed plan with actual facts. Each time a plan is handed to another party, the recipient will analyze the facts to confirm that the plan is correct, or to state any necessary correction; for example, the recipient may see that the other party's assumptions about the means required or the results attainable are not accurate. Through consensus a plan is finalized.

Until catchball is completed a plan cannot properly be deployed. In fact, it is usually best to finish catchball at one level before moving to another level of planning. The deployment team's side of the catchball step is described in the sequence of that team's activities, beginning on p. 101.

Step 4. Finalize Budgets

In Step 5 of the previous chapter, the focus team estimated the financial impacts of critical key and control points. It may also have prepared detailed budgets linked to the company's overall profit plans. At this stage in the deployment process, the focus team has handed off its Proposed Deployment Plans to the deployment teams, and the deployment teams have evaluated those plans, determined critical checkpoints, and played catchball with the focus team and any other teams involved. Having heard the criticisms and recommendations of the deployment teams, the focus team can now grasp the implications of its strategic planning on the allocation of company resources. The focus team may now finalize those budgets, after making any recommended adjustments in the specific critical keys and control points or in estimates of financial impacts.

Step 5. Summarize

The last step in the focus team's Standardization activities is to use the finalized Deployment Plans from each deployment team to update the Plan Summary document begun during the Focus phase. The revised Plan Summary will show the checkpoints and targets agreed to during catchball (see Figure 6-2 showing the revised Nonesuch Plan Summary). The Plan Summary provides a concrete reference for top management, middle management, and supervisors and helps highlight gaps between targeted and actual performance. The focus team completes the Plan Summary at the end of the Adherence phase of the Strategic Improvement Cycle.

DEPLOYMENT TEAM ACTIVITIES

In this section we will back up and take a look at what the deployment teams do during this phase. After the CEO launches the annual policy and convenes the deployment teams, the teams participate in the following steps:

1. Collect, analyze, and evaluate data
2. Determine critical checkpoints
3. Play catchball
4. Write Action Plans

Some of these steps have been written about from the focus team's perspective in the preceding sections; here we will focus on what the deployment teams actually do.

Step 1. Collect, Analyze, and Evaluate Data

Using the information on the Proposed Deployment Plans transmitted by the focus team, each deployment team sets up a Target/Means Diagram for each control point it has been assigned. The deployment teams enter gap

Nonesuch Casting Co.

Plan Summary (Revised)

Date:

Critical Keys	Control Points/ Checkpoints	Item #	Owner	Strategy	Target	Actual	Start	Complete	Notes
Leadership									
	Business Renewal	**2**	**President**	Lean Mgt. System	Done by:		10/1/95		
		2.1	"	Development Plan	12/1/95		10/1/95		
	Focus	2.2	**Marketing manager**	Annual Policy	1/1/96		12/1/95		
	Standardization	2.3	**President**	Action Plan	2/1/96		1/1/96		
	Adherence	2.4a	**Production manager**	Self-Reports	3/1/96		2/1/96		
		2.4b	"	Corporate Diagnosis	11/1/96		10/1/96		
	Reflection	2.5	**President**	Analysis Summary	12/1/96		11/1/96		
Lean equipment management		**8**	**Engineering manager**	Model equipment	OEE = 70%		1/1/96		
	Equip./process impr.	**8.1**	**Engineering manager**	Model equipment	OEE = 70%				
	Availability	8.1.1	Production coord./Maint. mgr.				1/1/96		
	Reduce breakdowns	*8.1.1a*	*Production coord./Maint. mgr.*	Model equipment	reduce 4%				
	Reduce changeover time	*8.1.1b*	*Production coord./Maint. mgr.*	Model equipment	30 min.		1/1/96		
	Performance efficiency	8.1.2	Engineering manager						
	Reduce minor stoppages	*8.1.2a*	*Eng. manager/Toolroom coord.*	Model equipment	study		1/1/96		
	Quality	8.1.3	Eng. manager/Production mgr.						
	Reduce cracking	*8.1.3a*	*Eng. manager/Production mgr.*	Model equipment	reduce 25%		1/1/96		
	Reduce warmups	*8.1.3b*	*Eng. manager/Production mgr.*	Model equipment	reduce 25%		1/1/96		
	Autonomous maint.	**8.2**	**Production mgr./Maint. mgr.**	1st 3 steps of AM	pilot		1/1/96		
	Initial cleaning	8.2.1	Maintenance manager	Step 1	major lines		1/1/96		
	Sources of dirt	8.2.2	Maintenance technician	Step 2	pilot		5/1/96		
	Establish basic stds.	8.2.3	Maintenance manager	Step 3	pilot		9/1/96		
	Safety	**8.3**	**Production manager**	DuPont program	LTA down 50%		1/1/96		
	Initial audit	8.3.1	Production manager	DuPont program	by 2/1/96		1/1/96		
	Establish standards	8.3.2	Production coordinator	On-Job-Training	all depts		6/1/96		

FIGURE 6-2.
REVISED PLAN SUMMARY

statements, target statements, and performance target graphs on their diagrams (in this case, as previously mentioned, the gap and target are the same as for the entire lean equipment management key). Next, the teams meet to discuss and confirm their understanding of each point in the Deployment Plans, and to organize for collecting relevant background facts pertaining to the gaps and targets described in the Plans. The object is to fully understand the performance each plan requires from the teams, so they should ask the focus team to clarify anything they don't understand. Figure 6-3 shows a diagram from Nonesuch Casting for the *equipment/process improvement* control point.

Information pertaining to gaps and targets may be available in the form of regular reports compiled by functional experts within the company. The deployment teams should obtain any such reports, and team members should analyze them in the light of the Proposed Deployment Plans. If such information it is not available, the team should organize research projects to collect and analyze it. Typical projects might include reading industry journals to learn about changes in markets or advances in technology, interviewing shopfloor employees to study attitudes towards work, or conducting time-motion studies of critical processes.

Once team members have compiled and analyzed this information, the team should reconvene to evaluate its analysis and then to confirm the gaps and targets specified in the Deployment Plans. If it appears that the focus team's expectations or understanding of the facts make a plan unrealistic, the deployment team should probably jump to a round of catchball (Step 3) before putting in the work involved in Step 2.

Step 2. Determine Critical Checkpoints

Implementation of policy requires targets and measures that correspond to the policy's strategic intent. Throughout the Business Renewal Process and the early steps of the Strategic Improvement Cycle, we have seen how the company vision can be translated into cascading levels of means to reach that ultimate target—from vision, to development plan, to annual policy theme and targets, to critical keys and critical control points. In this step, the deployment teams break down each critical control point into a set of critical checkpoints—the specific areas in which improvement actions will be applied and results will be measured.

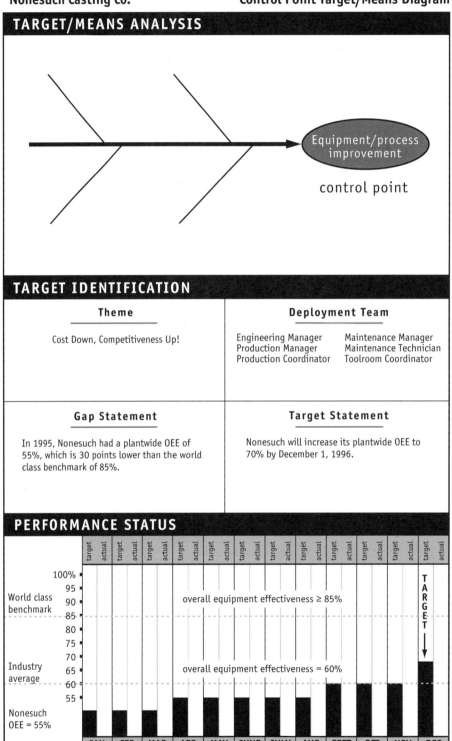

Checkpoints often represent critical process-related factors that contribute to or hinder control over operational objectives. Checkpoints help deployment and action teams evaluate performance toward targets and trigger corrective action. To select critical checkpoints to track, the deployment team can use brainstorming or relations diagrams to generate a list of possibilities. The team then prioritizes the checkpoints using a ranking matrix for effectiveness and efficiency, the same technique used to select the critical keys and control points (see p. 75 in Chapter 5). If sufficient quantitative data are available, the team can use Pareto analysis for this ranking. After selecting the checkpoints, the deployment team enters them as means on the fishbone diagram at the top of the target/means diagram. Figure 6-4 shows the Nonesuch Control Point Target/Means Matrix with three critical checkpoints identified .

In some cases, checkpoints for certain control points are already well defined by best practice. For example, when the engineering manager at Nonesuch deployed the *equipment/process improvement* control point, the principles and practice of total productive maintenance (TPM) made it clear that the checkpoints should be *equipment availability, performance efficiency,* and *product/process quality*—the three elements of the well-known overall equipment effectiveness (OEE) measure. These items appear as checkpoints in Figure 6-4.

Finally, the deployment team prepares an X-Type Matrix for each critical key, entering critical control points, critical checkpoints, and the team members who own each checkpoint. Figure 6-5 shows the X-Type Matrix created by Nonesuch Casting's LEMI deployment team.

Step 3. Play Catchball

The catchball process, introduced in the context of the focus team's Step 3 (p. 96), is the deployment team's opportunity to give feedback to the focus team about the Proposed Deployment Plans, and to ask for any changes it feels are necessary based on its review of the facts. The focus team must then respond to these considerations before the deployment teams will confirm the plan and launch the Deployment Plans.

Among the items reported back to top management in the catchball process is the deployment team's assessment of the resources required for the successful implementation of the Proposed Deployment Plans. Such

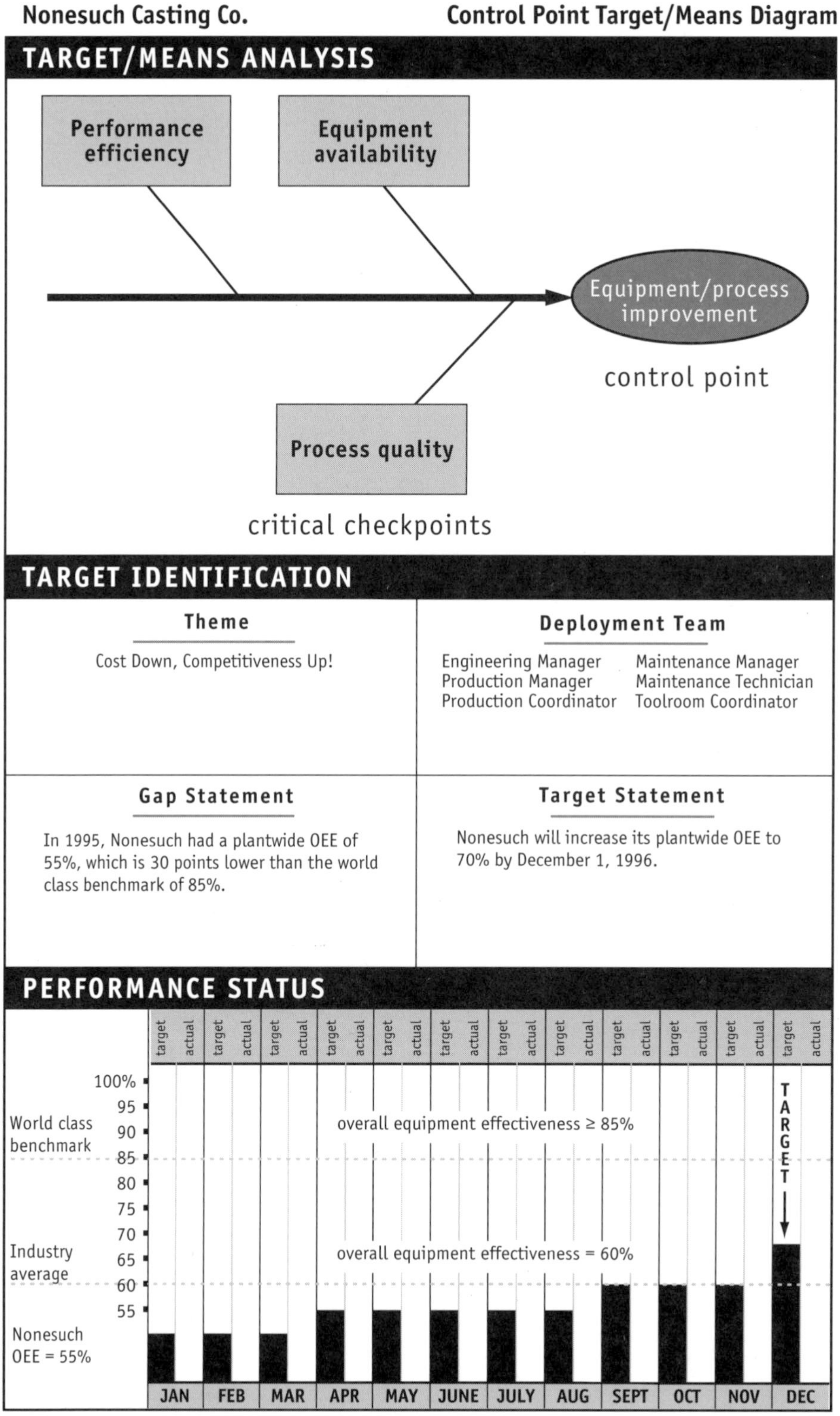

Nonesuch Casting Co.   **Control Point Target/Means Diagram**

TARGET/MEANS ANALYSIS

Performance efficiency	Equipment availability

Equipment/process improvement

control point

Process quality

critical checkpoints

TARGET IDENTIFICATION

Theme	Deployment Team	
Cost Down, Competitiveness Up!	Engineering Manager Production Manager Production Coordinator	Maintenance Manager Maintenance Technician Toolroom Coordinator

Gap Statement	Target Statement
In 1995, Nonesuch had a plantwide OEE of 55%, which is 30 points lower than the world class benchmark of 85%.	Nonesuch will increase its plantwide OEE to 70% by December 1, 1996.

PERFORMANCE STATUS

World class benchmark

overall equipment effectiveness ≥ 85%

100%
95
90
85
80
75
70
65
60
55

Industry average

overall equipment effectiveness = 60%

Nonesuch OEE = 55%

TARGET

JAN FEB MAR APR MAY JUNE JULY AUG SEPT OCT NOV DEC

FIGURE 6-4.
DEPLOYMENT TEAM TARGET/MEANS DIAGRAM
SHOWING CHECKPOINTS

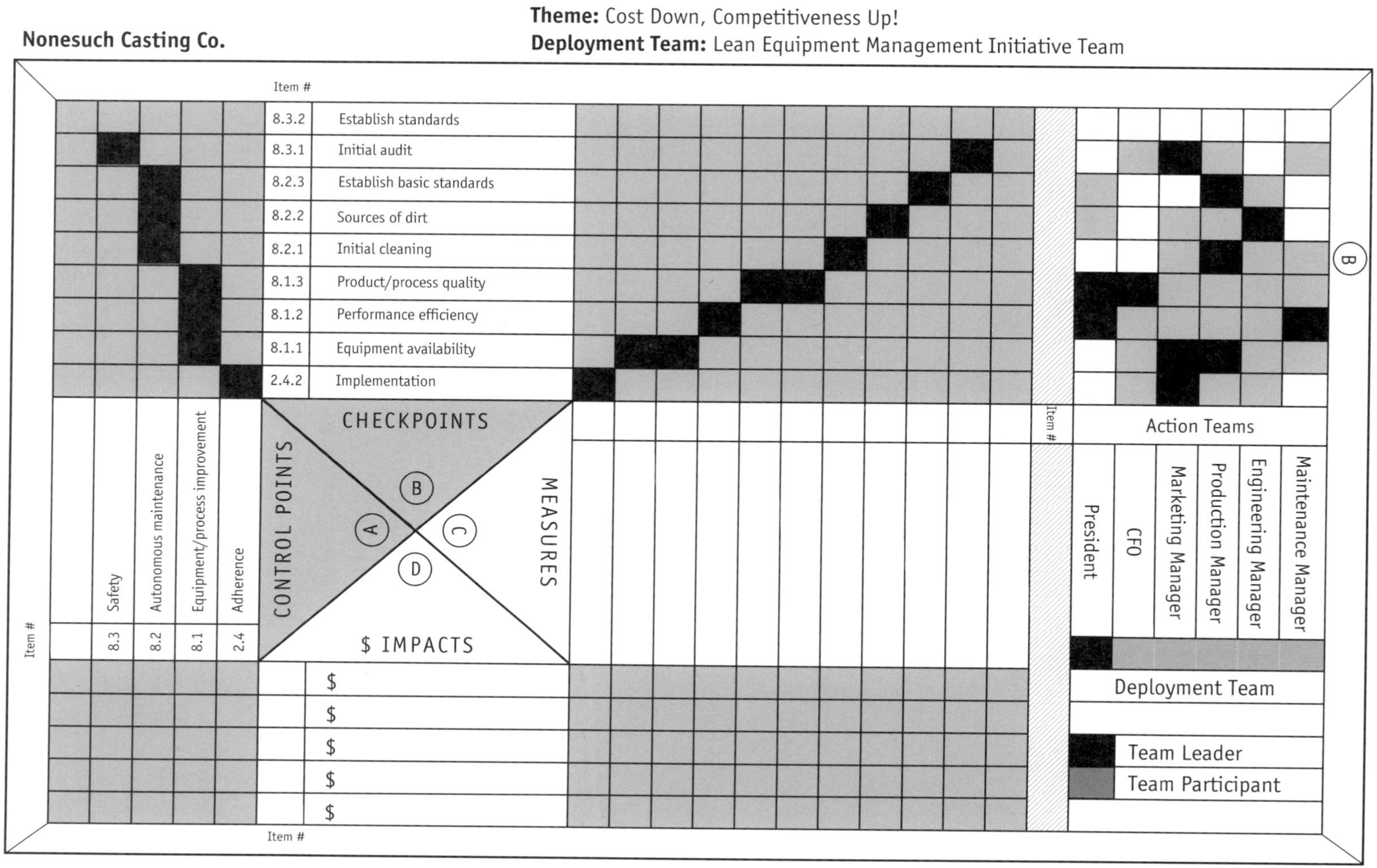

Nonesuch Casting Co.

Theme: Cost Down, Competitiveness Up!
Deployment Team: Lean Equipment Management Initiative Team

Action Teams:
- Maintenance Manager
- Engineering Manager
- Production Manager
- Marketing Manager
- CFO
- President

Deployment Team
- Team Leader
- Team Participant

Item #

MEASURES

CHECKPOINTS

$ IMPACTS

CONTROL POINTS

A B C D

Checkpoints (Item #):
- Establish standards — 8.3.2
- Initial audit — 8.3.1
- Establish basic standards — 8.2.3
- Sources of dirt — 8.2.2
- Initial cleaning — 8.2.1
- Product/process quality — 8.1.3
- Performance efficiency — 8.1.2
- Equipment availability — 8.1.1
- Implementation — 2.4.2

Control Points:
- Adherence — 2.4
- Equipment/process improvement — 8.1
- Autonomous maintenance — 8.2
- Safety — 8.3

Item #

$
$
$
$
$

FIGURE. 6-5.
DEPLOYMENT TEAM X-TYPE MATRIX SHOWING CONTROL POINTS AND CHECKPOINTS

resources might include new equipment, extra personnel, consultants, training, travel release time to work on special projects, and organizational changes. The focus team may have some awareness of such requirements when drafting the Proposed Deployment Plans, but will not have the specific information from deeper within the organization. The deployment teams provide this information to the focus team during catchball to get confirmation that the required resources will be made available.

In its review of the Proposed Deployment Plans, the deployment teams also consider the coordination of improvement activities in each department, cross-functional team, and workteam. The deployment teams specify for the focus team the activities that require cross-functional coordination, such as corrective action, process improvements, product development, internal communications, customer or supplier relations, and performance measurement.

This is also the time for deployment teams to suggest to the policy making team their own ideas for improving company policy and reaching overall objectives.

Step 4. Write and Transmit Action Plans

The deployment team assigns each member responsibility for implementing one or more checkpoints. Working as a group, the deployment team prepares for implementation by filling out Action Plans. The Action Plans are where the Deployment Plan targets are translated into manageable goals for each checkpoint. Each Action Plan should contain enough information to permit team leaders or supervisors to set up their own Target/Means Diagrams for actual implementation. In the next part of Phase II these diagrams will be analyzed and acted on by frontline-level small groups called action teams.

Figure 6-6 shows an Action Plan developed by the Nonesuch LEMI deployment team for the critical checkpoint *equipment availability*. Improvement in equipment availability will be measured by changeover time. The deployment team wants to reduce the changeover time to below 30 minutes, a big step toward the world class level of changeovers in under 10 minutes.

Like the Deployment Plan, the Action Plan contains many of the elements of the Target/Means Diagram, but on a more detailed level. It includes a concise statement on how the checkpoints will contribute to attaining and maintaining the control point target. A checkpoint "gap" is

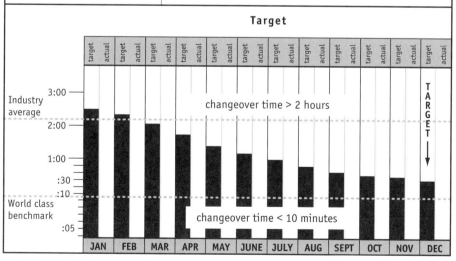

Action Plan

Nonesuch Casting Co.
Key: Lean equipment management
Control point: Equipment process improvement
Checkpoint: Equipment availability: Changeover time
Item #: 8.1.1b
Item Owner: Production Coordinator

Theme: Cost Down, Competitiveness Up!

Unit: Production Dept.
Date Updated:
Next Review:
Review Team:

Gap Statement

During the past year, Nonesuch has experienced long changeover times of greater than 2 hours per changeover throughout the plant. As a result, overall equipment effectiveness is low and costs are too high.

Target Statement

Nonesuch will reduce changeover times on all equipment to an average time of 30 minutes per changeover by October 1, 1996.

Core Objectives

The core objectives are to reduce changeover times to increase OEE and achieve greater production flexibility.

In addition, we have learned that quick changeover is a relatively simple technique. A quick return on training investment is expected. And it will also raise team morale. We hope this will reflect well on the TPM effort and support union buy-in.

Suggested Strategies

Conduct initial pilot training in SMED on 800-ton press in Team Leader 1's area.

Aim for dramatic breakthrough of 80% reduction in changeover times. Then stabilize gains by training all shifts and implementing controls.

To deploy SMED across the organization, from a network of changeover teams and conduct large-scale SMED training.

Target

Industry average

changeover time > 2 hours

3:00
2:00
1:00
:30
:10

World class benchmark

changeover time < 10 minutes

:05

| JAN | FEB | MAR | APR | MAY | JUNE | JULY | AUG | SEPT | OCT | NOV | DEC |

FIGURE 6-6.
AN ACTION PLAN

stated in terms of a problem that requires a solution, and the gap is pictured on a performance graph. The deployment teams determine a performance measure and set a target for each checkpoint, including the time frame for performance and important improvement milestones. If financial targets for control points have not been established by higher management, the deployment team also estimates the financial impact of successfully addressing each control point. However, the deployment team should refrain from dictating specific improvement ideas, which might discourage employee participation in implementation.

The deployment team enters the measures and financial impacts for each critical checkpoint on its X-Type Matrix; Figure 6-7 shows the Nonesuch example. (In this case the matrix shows the same numbers for the OEE target [Item 8.1] as in the Annual Policy X-Type Matrix [Figure 5-13] because this deployment team's equipment improvement activities are the company's major effort toward this target. However, other teams are also working toward the safety targets, so this team's savings in that category are less than the total estimated savings on that item in the Annual Policy matrix.)

After completing its X-Type Matrix, the deployment team submits the matrix and Action Plans to the focus team for use in revising and updating the Plan Summary. Finally, the deployment team kicks off the Implementation phase by giving the Action Plans to the assigned owners of each checkpoint—typically the midlevel managers on the deployment team—who will use them to initiate concrete improvement projects through small group activities across the company.

IMPLEMENTATION ACTIVITIES BY ACTION TEAMS

At the implementation level, the Deployment Plans' critical control points become the targets of Action Plans, with the measures for each critical checkpoint suggesting the means to be used to reach these targets. (The actual means used to attain each measure—the methodology and approach—are left to the action teams to determine, as will be explained in this section.) The end result of this cascading sequence of cause-and-effect is a complete lean management control structure—a system of goals, targets, means, and measures adapted to the requirements of every employee's daily work.

Actual implementation requires first the formation of action teams to manage the improvement activities in each workcenter. The action team is

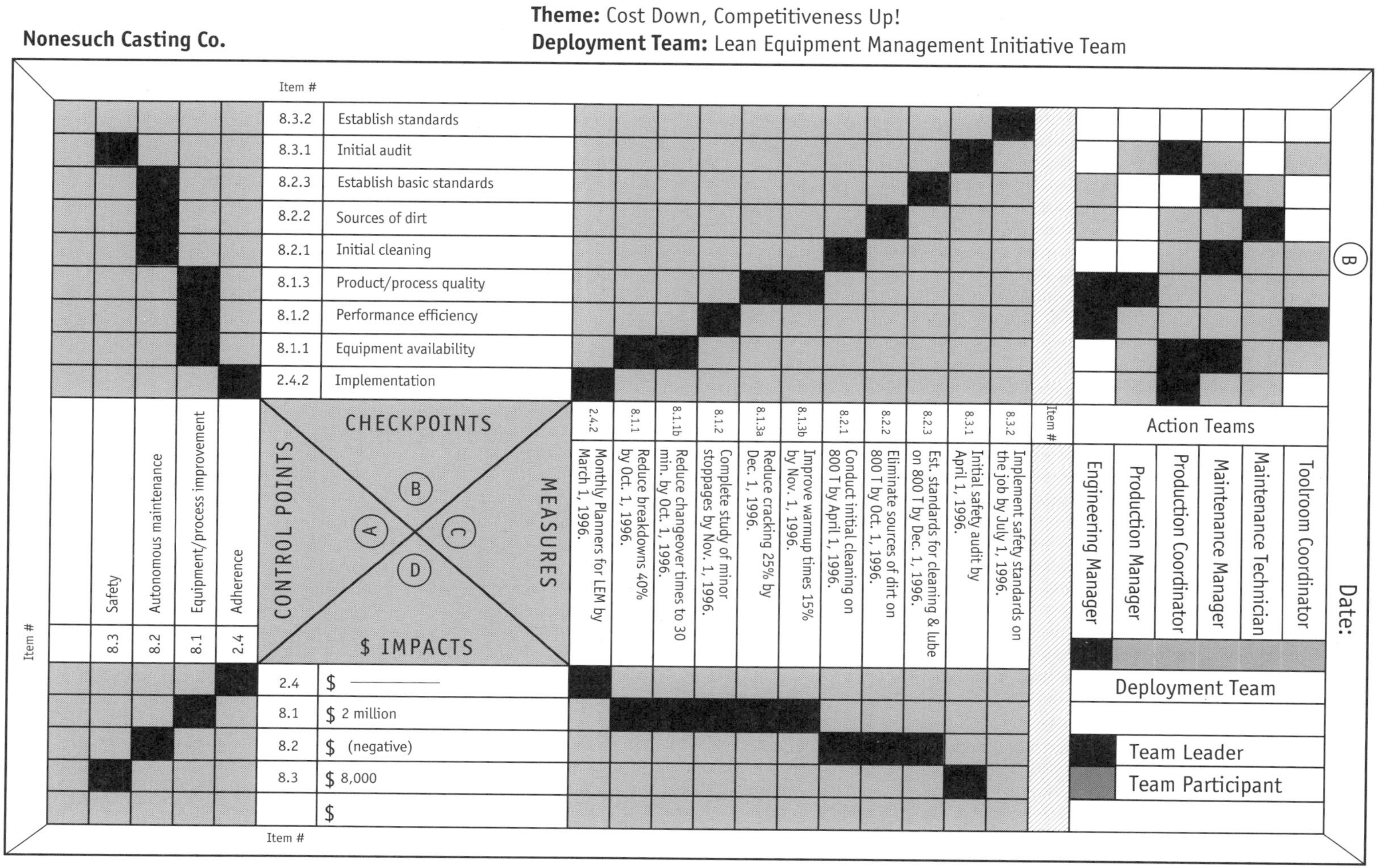

Nonesuch Casting Co.

Theme: Cost Down, Competitiveness Up!
Deployment Team: Lean Equipment Management Initiative Team

Ⓑ

Date:

Action Teams
- Toolroom Coordinator
- Maintenance Technician
- Maintenance Manager
- Production Coordinator
- Production Manager
- Engineering Manager

Deployment Team
Team Leader
Team Participant

Item #

Item #	
8.3.2	Implement safety standards on the job by July 1, 1996.
8.3.1	Initial safety audit by April 1, 1996.
8.2.3	Est. standards for cleaning & lube on 800 T by Dec. 1, 1996.
8.2.2	Eliminate sources of dirt on 800 T by Oct. 1, 1996.
8.2.1	Conduct initial cleaning on 800 T by April 1, 1996.
8.1.3b	Improve warmup times 15% by Nov. 1, 1996.
8.1.3a	Reduce cracking 25% by Dec. 1, 1996.
8.1.2	Complete study of minor stoppages by Nov. 1, 1996.
8.1.1b	Reduce changeover times to 30 min. by Oct. 1, 1996.
8.1.1	Reduce breakdowns 40% by Oct. 1, 1996.
2.4.2	Monthly Planners for LEM by March 1, 1996.

MEASURES

CHECKPOINTS   Ⓒ   Ⓑ   Ⓓ   Ⓐ $ IMPACTS

CONTROL POINTS

Item #	
8.3.2	Establish standards
8.3.1	Initial audit
8.2.3	Establish basic standards
8.2.2	Sources of dirt
8.2.1	Initial cleaning
8.1.3	Product/process quality
8.1.2	Performance efficiency
8.1.1	Equipment availability
2.4.2	Implementation

$ IMPACTS	Item #
$ ———	2.4
$ 2 million	8.1
$ (negative)	8.2
$ 8,000	8.3
$	

Control Points	Item #
Adherence	2.4
Equipment/process improvement	8.1
Autonomous maintenance	8.2
Safety	8.3

Item #

FIGURE 6-7.
DEPLOYMENT TEAM X-TYPE MATRIX SHOWING CHECKPOINT MEASURES AND FINANCIAL IMPACTS

led by the deployment team member—usually a midlevel departmental or area manager—to whom the Action Plan was assigned. Other members of the action team include the team leaders or supervisors, who will direct the workcenter improvement activities and support workteam members toward group and individual goals they will set. (If team leaders have been included on the deployment teams, they will serve as the leaders of the action teams. In that case the workteams become the action teams, and they work from the actual Action Plan rather than from the Implementation Plan discussed in a later section.)

Although we are focusing on equipment improvements in our example, action team activities are not limited to the shop floor. Staff support departments and even the president's office will follow the same procedure for implementing assigned items in the annual policy.

The action team's first task is to develop a specific schedule for meeting lean management Action Plan targets in each workcenter. Next, implementation requires the integration of goals and targets with the normal goals and targets of the company's daily work. Project teams, workteams, and individual employees then become involved, setting group and personal goals and targets, in alignment with the company's strategy and resources. Finally, everyone in the company—from the executive suite to the production line to the drafting room—begins the creative work of learning and improvement. In sequence, the steps are as follows:

1. Draw up workcenter plans
2. Assign targets for workteams
3. Set personal targets
4. Apply reliable methods to improve current standards

Step 1. Draw up Workcenter Plans

The area or departmental manager (the midlevel management member of the deployment team to whom the Action Plan was assigned) meets with individual team leaders or supervisors to establish the purpose of activities in each workcenter. They go over the strengths and weaknesses of each workteam in the workcenter and discuss the details of improvement targets for the next 12 months. The area manager and team leaders create Implementation Planning Sheets that convert Lean Management System control points and checkpoints into specific target-related activities for the workteams and managers. Together they plot out start and completion dates, showing them as open triangles on the plan. During the Adherence phase, the area manager will use this chart to track progress in all the Action Plans in which he or she is involved. As activities are begun and completed, the manager will blacken the appropriate triangles, or will color them red to show delays (see Figure 7-3 on p. 126 for a preview). Figure 6-8 shows the Implementation Planning Sheet for Nonesuch Casting checkpoints to be managed by the production coordinator.

Once the area manager and team leaders have finalized the annual workcenter plan, they make an enlarged version of the planning sheet and post it in the workcenter where all the workteams can see it. This Workcenter Control Board may take the form of a paper chart, or it might be a whiteboard using dry-erase markers and magnetic symbols. A paper chart is available from the publisher (see p. 33).

The Control Board communicates to team members the unit's current targets and strategies and team responsibilities for various targets. Its visual presentation of information creates a shared spirit of improvement among everyone in the workcenter. The implementation schedule becomes the focal point of daily meetings, giving valuable feedback to team leaders and area managers and speeding problem resolution.

At this point, the area managers and team leaders also explore together what methods they will apply to improve performance toward the targets. Area managers and team leaders can carry Idea Bank forms to jot down improvement ideas as they occur (see Figure 6-9 for an example). The Idea Banks become a useful resource for the workteams during implementation.

Step 2. Assign Targets and Tasks for Workteams

Next, each team leader meets with his or her workteam to explain the activities in which they will be involved and set targets for each team. Using the Workcenter Control Board, the leader and team members discuss the targets from each Action Plan and determine how to translate them into activities for the workteam. Each team prepares a set of Team Action Plans, describing activities and charting monthly target performance levels in each

Implementation Plan
Theme: Cost Down, Competitiveness Up!
Date:

Department: Production
Work Area: Workcenter 1
Area Manager: Production Coordinator

Nonesuch Casting Company

Critical Key	Control Points/Checkpoints	#	Owner	Strategy	Target	Actual	Start	Complete	1	2	3	4	5	6	7	8	9	10	11	12
Leadership	Adherence	2.4	Production mgr.																	
		2.4.1	Production coord.	Monthly review	planner		2/1/96	3/1/96		△	△									
			Team leader 1		planner		2/1/96	3/1/96		△	△									
			Team leader 2		planner		2/1/96	3/1/96		△	△									
			Team leader 3		planner		2/1/96	3/1/96		△	△									
			Team leader 4		planner		2/1/96	3/1/96		△	△									
			Team leader 5		planner		2/1/96	3/1/96		△	△									
		2.4.2	Production coord.		planner		2/1/96	3/1/96		△	△									
			Team leader 1		planner		2/1/96	3/1/96		△										
Lean equip. mgt.	Equip./process impr.	8.1	Eng. manager	Total Prod. Maint.	OEE = 70%		3/1/96	11/1/96											△	
	Availability	8.1.1																		
	Changeover time	8.1.1b	Production coord.	Adopt SMED	30 min.		3/1/96	10/1/96		△	△							△		
			Team leader 1		30 min.		3/1/96	10/1/96			△							△		
			Team leader 2		30 min.		3/1/96	10/1/96			△							△		
			Team leader 5		30 min.		3/1/96	10/1/96			△							△		
	Performance efficiency	8.1.2																		
	Minor stoppages	8.1.2a	Production coord.		study		3/1/96	11/1/96		△	△								△	
			Team leader 2		study		3/1/96	11/1/96		△	△								△	
			Team leader 3		study		3/1/96	11/1/96			△								△	
			Team leader 4		study		3/1/96	11/1/96			△									△
	Autonomous maint.	8.2	Production mgr.	Autonomous maint.	Steps 1–3		3/1/96	12/1/96												△
	Initial cleaning	8.2.1	Production coord.	....	clean		3/1/96	4/1/96			△	△								
			Team leader 1		clean		3/1/96	4/1/96			△	△								
			Team leader 2		clean		3/1/96	4/1/96				△	△							
	Sources of dirt	8.2.2	Production coord.	....	elim. dirt		5/1/96	10/1/96					△					△		
			Team leader 1		elim. dirt		5/1/96	10/1/96					△					△		
			Team leader 2		elim. dirt		5/1/96	10/1/96					△							
	Establish standards	8.3.2	Production coord.		est. stds.		9/1/96	12/1/96									△			△
			Team leader 1		est. stds.		9/1/96	12/1/96									△			△
	Safety	8.3	Production mgr.	DuPont program	OJT/audit		3/1/96	7/1/96							△					
	Initial audit	8.3.1	Production coord.	....	OJT/audit		3/1/96	4/1/96			△	△								
			Team leader 1		OJT/audit		3/1/96	4/1/96			△	△								
			Team leader 2		OJT/audit		3/1/96	4/1/96			△	△								
			Team leader 3		OJT/audit		3/1/96	4/1/96			△	△								
			Team leader 4		OJT/audit		3/1/96	4/1/96			△	△								
	Establish standards	8.3.2			est. stds.		6/1/96	7/1/96						△	△					
			Team leader 1		est. stds.		6/1/96	7/1/96						△	△					
			Team leader 2		est. stds.		6/1/96	7/1/96						△	△					
			Team leader 3		est. stds.		6/1/96	7/1/96						△	△					
			Team leader 4		est. stds.		6/1/96	7/1/96							△					

MONTH

FIGURE 6-8.
IMPLEMENTATION PLANNING SHEET

	Person	Material	Machine	Method	Measure	Information
Customer focus	take Mark to visit our customers		use the Internet to stay in touch			what are our customers thinking
Leadership	get Keith involved in initial cleaning			morning meetings for office staff	conduct Corporate Diagnosis	
Lean organization				establish co-makership program		
Information architecture		introduce kanban	how much is a good label maker?		post photos of model line improvements	
Culture of improvement	more employee involvement			CEDAC training for project leaders		books from Productivity Press
Lean production		supplier quality too variable				
Lean equipment management	Dennis to build hands-on training equip.		install quick-change fasteners	apply poka-yoke method	calculate OEE electronically	
Lean engineering		new alloys for lighter, stronger parts		engineering office on shop floor	what is our time to market?	study concurrent engineering

FIGURE 6-9.
A SAMPLE IDEA BANK

checkpoint assigned to the team. Figure 6-10 shows a sample Team Action Plan for one of the Nonesuch Casting workteams. (As mentioned before, in situations where the team leaders were on the deployment teams, the workteams will proceed directly from the deployment team's Action Plans and do not need to create separate Team Action Plans.)

Some Action Plans handed to the workteams are "closed-ended," meaning that they prescribe the specific means or methodologies the teams are to use as well as the targets. Workteams may begin action on closed-ended items immediately with little analysis or investigation. The Nonesuch equipment availability/ changeover time Action Plan (Figure 6-6 on p. 105) is an example of a closed-ended plan; it expects workteams to apply a specific methodology—SMED (single-minute exchange of dies)—to reduce changeover times.

On the other hand, if the Action Plan prescribes only the targets and measures but not the means of improvement, it is called "open-ended." In

Team Action Plan

Nonesuch Casting Co.
Checkpoint: Equipment availability: Changeover time
Item #: 8.1.1b
Item Owner: Team leader 1
Team/Dept: Team 1
Location: Plant 1

Theme: Cost Down, Competitiveness Up!

Date Updated:
Next Review:
Review Team:

Gap Statement

During the past year, Nonesuch has experienced long changeover times of greater than 2 hours per changeover throughout the plant. As a result, overall equipment effectiveness is low and costs are too high.

Target Statement

Nonesuch will reduce changeover times on all equipment to an average time of 30 minutes per changeover by October 1, 1996.

Core Objectives

The core objectives are to reduce changeover times to increase OEE and achieve greater production flexibility.

In addition, we have learned that quick changeover is a relatively simple technique. A quick return on training investment is expected. And it will also raise team morale.

Team Assignments

Task	Target Date
Complete SMED quick changeover training	2/28
Videotape and time baseline changeover on 800-ton press	3/3
Analyze internal and external changeover elements for 800-ton press	3/15
Plan improved changeover process for 800-ton press	3/15
Perform pilot run of improved changeover process	3/17
Plan and submit work orders for machine modifications, die transfer system, and changeover cart	4/15
Complete machine modifications for pilot implementation	4/30
Complete changeover cart	4/30
Build die transfer system	5/15
Time all changeovers, recording steps and circumstances that cause delay	ongoing
Continuously analyze changeovers for improvement possibilities	ongoing

Target

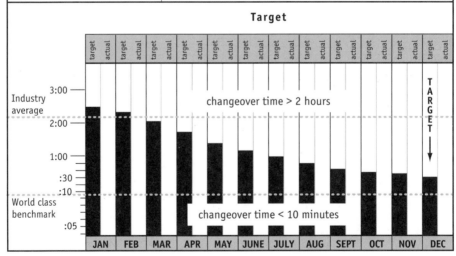

FIGURE 6-10.
A TEAM ACTION PLAN

that case, workteams determine their tasks by systematically analyzing the causes of the problem and identifying the means required to address those causes. If this analysis reveals major discrepancies between specified targets and the means currently available to the workteam, the team should engage in catchball with the action team that assigned the targets. The action team must either arrange for the necessary means or adjust the target expectations.

Step 3. Set Personal Targets and Tasks

Individual employees are expected to identify their own areas of concern related to workteam improvement targets and to think through their own improvement measures and methods. Each employee works with his or her team leader to establish personal goals based on the Workcenter Control Board. Together they fill out Monthly Planner forms to record these jointly developed goals. Figure 6-11 shows a Nonesuch example. At the end of each week, team members record their progress on the Self-Report form on the back of the Monthly Planner sheet (see blank Nonesuch example in Figure 6-12). At the end of each month, they will submit the form as a "report card" to their team leader, who summarizes team results for the action team (a completed form is shown in Chapter 7).

The team leader or supervisor also involves each employee in the workteam in setting personal goals on a daily basis. Employees use Daily Planner forms to remind themselves of daily, weekly, and monthly goals and assignments, and to record new learning and questions along the way (see Figure 6-13 on p. 116).

During the initial months of activities, each employee takes some time at the end of the shift to review his or her improvement-related performance for the day, compared with the goals and assignments in the Monthly Planner. The employee then sets a new assignment for the following day, recording it in the "Special Tasks" section of the next day's Daily Planner form. The employee passes the current and following days' Planner forms to the team leader for review. The team leader returns them to the employee with appropriate comments, adjustments, and suggestions during regular meetings each morning. Once the improvement system gets established in the workcenters, the reporting, feedback, and improvement assignments can all take place during the morning meeting, with employees referring to their Daily Planners for points to raise in team discussion.

Monthly Planner	
Employee: Operator 1 – Production Department	
Current Month	**Next Month**
March	**April**
Goal: To reduce changeover times on 800-ton press to below 30 minutes.	Goals: To maintain changeover reductions. Make equipment modifications to speed change of dies.
1	1
2	2
3 SUNDAY	3
4 Videotape changeover on 800 T press	4
5	5
6	6
7	7 SUNDAY
8	8
9 Study video at home	9
10 SUNDAY	10
11 Attend safety training	11
12 Attend safety training	12
13	13
14	14 SUNDAY
15	15
16 Team separates internal from external setup	16
17 SUNDAY	17
18 Perform changeovers according to new standard	18
19 Study ways to switch internal to external setup	19
20	20
21	21 SUNDAY
22	22
23 Time new changeovers	23
24 SUNDAY	24
25	25
26	26
27	27
28	28 SUNDAY
29 Turn in monthly report	29
30	30
31 SUNDAY	31

FIGURE 6-11.
A MONTHLY PLANNER FORM

| Self-Report |

Employee: Operator 1 – Production Dept.   **Month:** _____

IMPROVEMENT AREA: Kaizen reporting

MEASURE: Implemented suggestions/week
TARGET: 1 suggestion/week

week   week   week   week
  1   2   3   4

Problems

IMPROVEMENT AREA: Equipment/process
                          improvement
MEASURE: Changeover time (minutes)
TARGET: 30 minutes on 800-ton press

week   week   week   week
  1   2   3   4

Problems

IMPROVEMENT AREA: Safety

MEASURE: Reportable incidents
TARGET: Zero incidents

Problems

IMPROVEMENT AREA:

MEASURE:
TARGET:

Problems

FIGURE 6-12.
A MONTHLY SELF-REPORT FORM

Daily Planner

Employee: Operator 1 – 800 T Press

Date: _March 28_____

Reminders	Special Tasks
1. Weekly lubrication check	Paint location marks on nuts on the press tonight.
2. Monthly Report due tomorrow	Use epoxy paint stored in toolroom. See Toolroom
3. Update Workcenter Control Board	Coordinator. Maintenance will tighten bolts
	correctly, then paint.

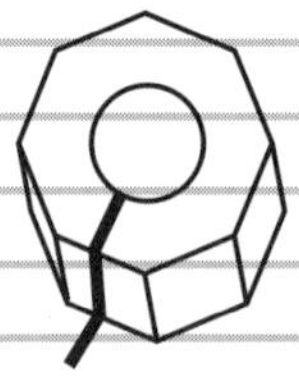

When the location marks line up, no problem.

When they don't line up, there's a problem.

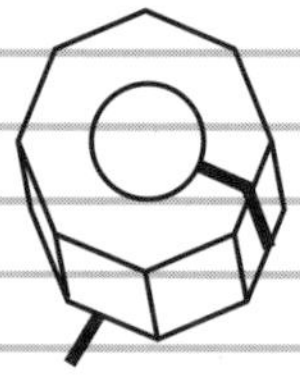

Wedding anniversary next week: buy present!

Points to Raise in Daily Meetings

FIGURE 6-13.
A DAILY PLANNER FORM

Step 4. Apply Reliable Methods and Improve Current Standards

The actual improvement activity is now carried out by the employees responsible for each checkpoint. Workteams will often be assigned projects for which they must improvise specific tasks and performance measures. In many cases, workteams will become actively involved in translating checkpoints into concrete improvement activities that apply reliable methods—approaches known to yield improvement results. Major reliable methods include just-in-time, total productive maintenance, total quality management, CEDAC (cause-and-effect diagram with the addition of cards), and concurrent engineering. These methods incorporate many discrete approaches that can be combined as needed: control charts, the QC story, cell design and quick changeover techniques, visual control methods, mistake-proofing devices (poka-yoke), computer applications, and autonomation (automation with human interaction). In short, the team has at its disposal the entire battery of current best practices. At this stage, teams should review improvement approaches recorded in area managers' or team leaders' Idea Banks to avoid reinventing the wheel. Employees unfamiliar with the selected improvement approach need to receive training.

Involvement and implementation are virtually synonymous in a world class company. Through involvement in improvement activities, each employee acquires a personal interest in the strategic intent of the firm.

In traditional organizations, frontline workers are handed policy that may or may not be relevant, and expected to pull toward those goals trustingly and without much flak. This is an unrealistic expectation that wastes a critical company asset—process knowledge that exists only at the value-adding level of the workforce. The next chapter, "Adherence," explains how the Lean Management System prompts employees to report feedback on their improvement activities. This feedback can then flow back through the management structure to inform future policy making.

NOTES

1. Catchball is explained further in the introductory sections of Yoji Akao, *Hoshin Kanri: Policy Deployment for Successful TQM* (Portland, Ore.: Productivity Press, 1991), and in Shoji Shiba, Alan Graham, and David Walden, *A New American TQM: Four Practical Revolutions in Management* (Portland, Ore.: Productivity Press, 1993), pp. 433-34.

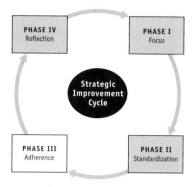

CHAPTER 7

Phase III: Adherence

THE ESSENCE OF THE ADHERENCE PHASE IS FOLLOW-UP of the companywide improvement activities begun in the Standardization phase. Follow-up is another shortcoming of a traditional strategic planning approach to improvement. Even if the company's improvement goals get as far as deployment and action at the work unit level, too often nothing happens to monitor progress. The next year, employees think "we tried it and it didn't work"—a sure way to kill involvement and learning.

Activities in the Adherence phase make sure everyone in the company, including top management, stays aware of improvement efforts and doesn't stop caring about the targets. These activities use a reporting system to send feedback through the management structure about what works, what does not, and what additional resources are needed to reach higher targets.[1] They also support dissemination and deployment of frontline employees' knowledge and improvement ideas throughout the company. Figure III-1 (page 62) summarizes team activities in Phase III.

ACTION TEAM ADHERENCE ACTIVITIES

The basic activities of the Adherence phase begin at the action team level. Adherence primarily consists of regular reporting from individual employees and work groups on progress toward improvement targets from the Action Plans and Workcenter Control Boards. Hence, Adherence actually happens in tandem with the application of improvement methods during the improvement cycle. Since it involves a sequence of interactions between various levels and functions of company management, it is useful to treat it as a separate phase.

Action team Adherence activities are not sequential steps, but things that are done in parallel over the course of the Strategic Improvement Cycle. They include the following:

- Create a visual information system
- Maintain a reporting system
- Support continuous learning in the workplace

Create a Visual Information System

Through the deployment process generally, and specifically by posting Workcenter Control Boards throughout the workplace and by involving workers directly in monthly and daily planning, management has communicated a new set of policy targets to the entire workforce. As they are achieved, these targets establish a new standard of performance for the company—the baseline for future improvements.

Successful adherence to new standards is founded on a shared understanding among the people expected to maintain the improvement. As improvements are made and standards are changed, it is easy to become confused and make errors. Lean companies use visual controls to enhance the information available in the workplace, quickly stabilizing situations in which new standards have been deployed.

Visual control methods are the building blocks of a *visual information system.* They are based on the idea of *just-in-time information*—the right information, in an appropriate form, in the hands of the people who can act on it, precisely when it is needed. The Workcenter Control Board itself is a visual control tool, sharing target dates and performance with everyone in the workplace. A visual information system takes a lot of information that was formerly locked away in a managerial office and builds it into the daily process on the shop floor. Mistake-proofing the work environment is one of its key uses.

We'll use machine lubrication for an example of how visual controls can be applied to prevent mistakes. In many factories machines break down because someone neglects to lubricate them or uses the wrong lubricant. Factors behind these errors include not having the information at hand that tells when to lubricate or what kind of lubricant to use. Visual controls can remedy many such workplace errors by making the information available, or even responding automatically to the need at hand. At a basic level, visual control for lubrication might mean placing a sticker near a machine's oil inlet telling employees how often to lubricate and which lubricant to use. Employees might even color-code the oil inlet to the lubricant containers to ensure that the right product is used. At a higher level, a machine might be modified so that it signals an operator or technician when lubricants reach critical levels—or even self-lubricates.

Other types of visual controls for mistake-proofing involve configuring machine jigs so that the workpiece cannot be processed backward or upside down. In addition to mistake-proofing, visual controls have many other applications in the production environment, such as floor marks showing where to place pallets (maintains orderly environment and enables visual check of inventory level), or where a door will swing (avoids accidents to employees, inventory, and equipment).

Visual controls have everything to do with empowering the workforce to do the right thing. Although little recognized in the West, *employee-developed* improvements like the ones just mentioned are a major factor in the consistent high quality and low cost enjoyed by major Japanese manufacturing companies. Companies must promote such open information sharing and mistake-proofing if they hope to maintain the performance levels it takes to compete with such lean producers. Key 5, *information architecture,* incorporates a lot of these approaches. See the resource list for other materials about visual controls and mistake-proofing.

Maintain a Reporting System

The Lean Management System uses several kinds of reporting to communicate information about improvement progress and obstacles, keeping the rest of the organization up to date, both vertically and laterally.

DAILY MEETINGS

At the workcenter level, workteams meet briefly each day with their team leaders. Daily meetings usually last ten to fifteen minutes and are conducted at the beginning or end of a shift. In these meetings, team leaders review work schedules and make any special assignments related to the work or the improvement process. If problems have arisen, the team leaders will learn about them and can take quick corrective action. The daily team meeting also provides a forum for sharing and testing out new improvement ideas. Following the team meetings, team leaders usually have a daily action team meeting with their area manager to share information upward. The area manager in turn will report results, problems, and new improvement ideas to the deployment team.

Self-reporting. As noted in Chapter 6, workteam members come to the daily meeting with their Daily and Monthly Planner forms and use them to bring up problems they have noted during the previous work period. They also use the backs of the forms to self-report. The back of the Daily Planner form contains a space for writing and sketching new improvement ideas as they occur (Figure 7-1 shows an example from Nonesuch Casting that was entered on the back of the Daily Planner in Figure 6-13).

As mentioned in Chapter 6, team members use the back of the Monthly Planner form to chart their weekly progress toward team and individual improvement targets. For example, Figure 7-2 (a filled-out version of Figure 6-12) shows graphs tracking the employee's implemented suggestions, changeover times, and safety information. These graphs and other data become a "report card" that gives employees and team leaders a sense of the progress made and impediments to be removed. At the end of the month, the employee hands the report card to his or her team leader. They discuss the results, then determine performance measures and targets for the coming month on a new card. In practice, the monthly report card should be customized to suit the company environment and the individual needs of each employee.

Workcenter Control Boards. The most immediate way of reporting adherence to the annual improvement policy is through visual display. In the Standardization phase, teams throughout the company posted critical keys, control points, checkpoints, and improvement targets on large wall charts called Workcenter Control Boards (area managers keep a form version of this

Improvement Ideas

Employee: Operator 1—Production   **Date:** March 28

Still having problems getting changeover times down on the 800 T Press. What we need is a quick change cart where all the tools we need for changeover are stored.

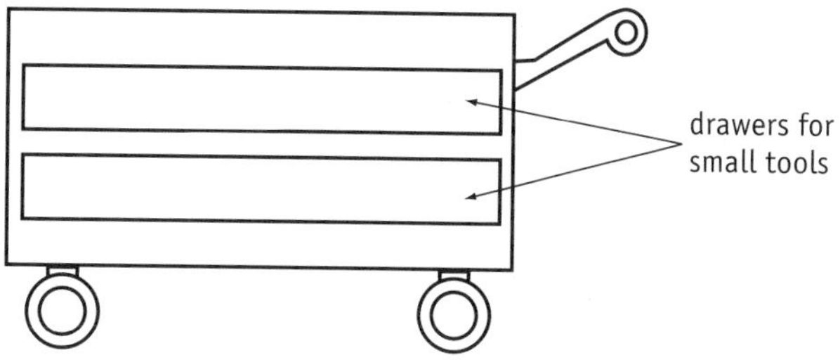

drawers for
small tools

We also need something to help the robot recognize good parts from bad ones. Maybe we need one of those poka-yoke devices I heard about at the last TPM training. Speak to the engineering manager. . .

FIGURE 7-1.
DAILY PLANNER FORM (REVERSE) FOR RECORDING
IMPROVEMENT IDEAS

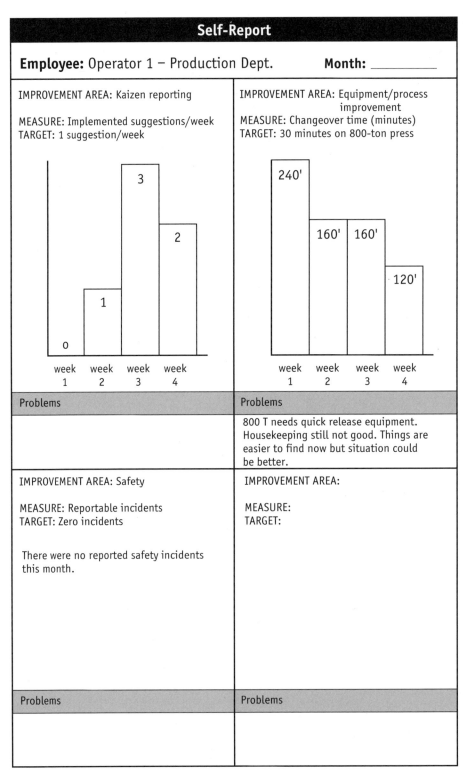

FIGURE 7-2.
MONTHLY SELF-REPORT FORM (EMPLOYEE "REPORT CARD")

chart, the Implementation Planning Sheet shown in Figure 6-8). A startup version of a Nonesuch Casting Workcenter Control Board was shown in Figure 2-8 on p. 35. Figure 7-3 (p. 126) shows the same Control Board as it might appear at the end of September. The chart on the right side of the control board uses triangles to mark the start and completion dates of activities for each checkpoint. The triangles are open when the control board is first prepared. During Adherence, the teams darken the triangles to indicate that they have started or completed activities on time. If a delay has occurred, the team uses a red triangle (shown here in gray) to indicate the holdup. This shared visual information makes it easy for everyone to verify the status of specific improvement activities at a glance. Figure 7-4 provides a visual key for the tracking symbols.

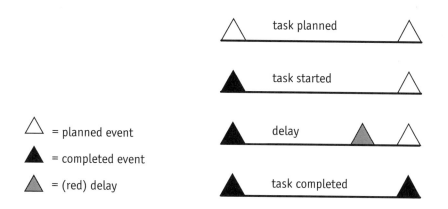

FIGURE 7-4.
SCHEDULE TRACKING SYMBOLS

Visual reporting on Workcenter Control Boards is a powerful technique to keep everyone in the company informed about the progress of policy implementation. It also provides managers with a simple tool for management-by-exception. In particular, reports of delays in implementation indicate areas for possible management intervention and assistance in problem solving.

For example, the control board in Figure 7-3 shows graphically that as of October 1, Nonesuch Production Teams 1 and 2 have reported delays in finishing item 8.2.2 (eliminating sources of dirt). In lieu of time-consuming formal reports, this simple charting device gives the area manager enough information to ask why such a delay has occurred and determine whether

Implementation Plan
Theme: Cost Down, Competitiveness Up!
Date:

Department: Production
Work Area: Workcenter 1
Area Manager: Production coordinator

Nonesuch Casting Company

Critical Key	Control/Check	#	Owner	Strategy	Target	Actual	Start	Complete	1	2	3	4	5	6	7	8	9	10	11	12
Leadership	**Adherence**	**2.4**	**Production mgr.**																	
		2.4.1	Production coord.	Monthly review	planner	planner	2/1/96	3/1/96		◄	◄									
			Team leader 1		planner	planner	2/1/96	3/1/96		◄	◄									
			Team leader 2		planner	planner	2/1/96	3/1/96		◄	△◄	◄								
			Team leader 3		planner	planner	2/1/96	3/1/96		◄	△△									
			Team leader 4		planner	planner	2/1/96	3/1/96		◄	△△	◄								
			Team leader 5		planner	planner	2/1/96	3/1/96		◄	◄									
		2.4.2	Production coord.		planner	planner	2/1/96	3/1/96		◄										
			Team leader 1		planner		2/1/96	3/1/96											△	
Lean equip. mgt.	**Equip./process impr.**	**8.1**	**Eng. manager**	Total Prod. Maint.	OEE = 70%		3/1/96	11/1/96			◄									
	Availability	8.1.1																		
	Changeover time	8.1.1b	Production coord.	Adopt SMED	30 min.	45 min.	3/1/96	10/1/96			◄		◄							
			Team leader 1		30 min.	30 min.	3/1/96	10/1/96			◄	◄	◄							
			Team leader 2		30 min.	50 min.	3/1/96	10/1/96			◄	◄								
			Team leader 5		30 min.	45 min.	3/1/96	10/1/96				◄								
	Performance efficiency	8.1.2																		
	Minor stoppages	8.1.2a	Production coord.		study		3/1/96	11/1/96			◄							△		
			Team leader 2		study		3/1/96	11/1/96			◄							△		
			Team leader 3		study		3/1/96	11/1/96			◄							△		
			Team leader 4		study	Steps 1–3	3/1/96	12/1/96			◄									△
	Autonomous maint.	**8.2**	**Production mgr.**	Autonomous maint.	Steps 1–3															
	Initial cleaning	8.2.1	Production coord.		clean	clean	3/1/96	4/1/96			◄	◄	◄							
			Team leader 1		clean	clean	3/1/96	4/1/96			◄	◄	◄							
			Team leader 2		clean	clean	3/1/96	4/1/96												
	Sources of dirt	8.2.2	Production coord.	··············	elim. dirt		5/1/96	10/1/96						◄				△△		
			Team leader 1		elim. dirt		5/1/96	10/1/96						◄				△△		
			Team leader 2		elim. dirt		5/1/96	10/1/96						◄				△△		
	Establish standards	8.3.2	Production coord.	··············	est. stds.		9/1/96	12/1/96									◄			△
			Team leader 1		est. stds.		9/1/96	12/1/96									◄			△
	Safety	**8.3**	**Production mgr.**	DuPont program	OJT/audit	OJT/audit	3/1/96	7/1/96			◄	◄	◄	◄	◄					
	Initial audit	8.3.1	Production coord.		OJT/audit	OJT/audit	3/1/96	4/1/96			◄	◄								
			Team leader 1		OJT/audit	OJT/audit	3/1/96	4/1/96			◄	△△								
			Team leader 2		OJT/audit	OJT/audit	3/1/96	4/1/96			◄	◄	◄							
			Team leader 3		OJT/audit	OJT/audit	3/1/96	4/1/96				△△								
			Team leader 4		OJT/audit	OJT/audit	3/1/96	4/1/96			◄									
	Establish standards	8.3.2	Team leader 1		est. stds.		6/1/96	7/1/96						◄	◄					
			Team leader 2		est. stds.		6/1/96	7/1/96						◄	◄					
			Team leader 3		est. stds.		6/1/96	7/1/96						◄	◄					
			Team leader 4		est. stds.		6/1/96	7/1/96						◄	◄					

MONTH

FIGURE 7-3.
WORKCENTER CONTROL BOARD SHOWING DELAYS AND COMPLETIONS

intervention will remove obstacles. Awareness of delays is particularly important in lean organizations, where interdependent improvement projects are managed cross-functionally throughout the company and delays in one area can halt progress in another.

WORKTEAMS' REPORTS TO THE ACTION TEAM

Team Action Plan. During Adherence, the workteams use the graphs on the bottom of each Team Action Plan to chart the actual month to month performance levels toward each target assigned to them. The team leaders share this information with their area manager during regular action team meetings and discuss solutions to any problems that have arisen.

AREA MANAGERS' REPORTS

The area managers track team information and summarize it for the deployment teams as necessary. The deployment teams serve as cross-functional advisors and resources for issues that arise during improvement activities.

Implementation Planning Sheet. During the course of the improvement cycle, each area manager maintains an Implementation Planning Sheet as a miniature version of the Workcenter Control Board, filling in triangles to match the wall chart. This provides a portable version of the wall chart information for use in discussions outside the workcenter, such as in reporting to the deployment team.

Analysis Sheets. During deployment, the deployment team developed Action Plans for each checkpoint and assigned ownership to various area managers. During Adherence, the area managers use an Analysis Sheet on the back of each Action Plan form to note the current status of top-priority implementation issues, as well as the individual owner who is working for resolution by a targeted date. This information is also relayed to the deployment team as necessary. Figure 7-5 shows an Analysis Sheet from the Nonesuch Casting example. Analysis Sheets may be supplemented by other quality management charts, including cause-and-effect diagrams, affinity diagrams, and so forth.

Status Reports. Based on the findings in the Analysis Sheets, the area managers prepare monthly two-page Status Reports to inform cross-functional team managers and department managers at the deployment team level. The purpose of the Status Report is to give a succinct account of

Action Plan Analysis Sheet

Nonesuch Casting Co.
Key: Lean equipment management
Control Point: Equipment/process improvement
Checkpoint: Equipment availability: Changeover time
Item #: 8.1.1b
Item Owner: Production Coordinator

Theme: Cost Down, Competitiveness Up!

Unit: Production Dept.
Date Updated:
Next Review:
Review Team:

Implementation Issues

Issue	Owner	Resolution/Date
800 T needs quick release equipment before changeover times can be brought beneath 120 minutes. Housekeeping to be improved.	Team leader 1	New clamps expected by May 30. Follow-up training on the 5S's scheduled for April 20.
Progress in low pressure area excellent. Housekeeping is much better, but there are problems in getting second and third shifts to follow the new changeover procedures.	Team leader 2	Conduct SMED training on second and third shifts before May 15.
There are still problems with scheduling. We need to know in advance when a changeover is going to occur so we can stage dies and changeover tools.	Production manager	Install weekly schedule on production control board by April 20.

FIGURE 7-5.
ACTION PLAN ANALYSIS SHEET FOR CHANGEOVER TIME

progress in implementing the annual improvement policy. Each statement in the report should be carefully documented; the area manager should be able to defend his or her conclusions with hard facts. The document should be short and concrete. Figure 7-6 on pp. 130–131 shows a sample Status Report for the Nonesuch Casting example.

Support Continuous Learning in the Workplace

Improvement activities in a world class organization require an attitude of Delta Zero—a willingness to see and act from a fresh perspective to reach performance levels not previously experienced. This attitude necessarily means continuous learning at the frontline level—about the current process, about new technology that can improve performance, about techniques that can make the current equipment or process perform better. Improvement in the critical keys often requires that workers acquire an expanded knowledge base, as well as a set of skills different from that required for daily production. Knowledge and skill training are therefore critical to the success of the improvement program.

The type of improvement training support needed will vary from one workcenter to another. Frontline employees should learn the basic steps of problem-solving and how to use the 7 QC tools to chart and analyze data. Beyond that, training may be tailored to the specific control points and checkpoints assigned to the workteam. For example, the Nonesuch teams who are trying to improve equipment availability by reducing changeover time should be trained in quick changeover techniques; for the autonomous maintenance control point, team members would start by learning how to do cleaning and inspection on their equipment. Demonstrations in pilot areas supplement employee training through visual examples.

Learning needs may change during the course of the Strategic Improvement Cycle. Team leaders and area managers need to be alert to this as they review employee self-reports and track performance toward the targets.

DEPLOYMENT TEAM ADHERENCE ACTIVITIES

The primary activity of the deployment team during the Adherence Phase is to manage a system for monthly analysis of the improvement data reported by the action teams (through the area manager's Action Plan

Status Report, page 1	Reporting Unit: Production Department/Action Team
Review Period:	*Area Manager:* Production coordinator
Control Point Goals Emphasized	**Concrete Steps**
1) Adherence	1) The Lean Management Monthly Planner has been introduced on the shop floor to promote Autonomous Maintenance activities. 2) Workcenter Control Boards have been set up in all workcenters, and team leaders and team members are updating them on a regular basis. 3)
2) Equipment/process improvement	1) Equipment availability has been improved 20% through reducing changeover time by 40% and breakdowns by 20%. 2) Equipment performance has been improved by 5% through the elimination of minor stoppages on some lines. 3) Product/process quality has been improved by 10% through improved warmups and by ongoing SQC.
3) Safety	1) All employees have received basic training in the DuPont Safety Program. 2) 3)
4)	1) 2) 3)

FIGURE 7-6.
AREA MANAGER'S STATUS REPORT

Results

3-Year Record (yearly average)

	Checkpoint	1993	1994	1995
8.3a	Lost time accidents	2	2	1
8.3b	Reported violations	15	24	9
8.1.1a	Breakdowns	24 hrs / week	20 hrs/week	19 hrs/ week
8.1.1b	Changeover time	2.5 hours	2.25 hours	2 hours
8.1.2a	Minor stoppages	not recorded	not recorded	10% capacity
8.1.3a	Cracked castings	1%	0.80%	0.75%
8.1.3b	Warmup times	1 hr/ warmup	1 hr / warmup	45 min./ warmup
2.4a.1	Monthly reports	N/A	N/A	N/A
2.4b.1	Control boards	N/A	N/A	N/A

This Period's Results

	Measure	Target	Performance	Comments
8.3a	Lost time accidents	zero	zero	
8.3b	Reported violations	5 / year	4 to date	
8.1.1a	Breakdowns	15 hrs / week	16 hrs / week	
8.1.1b	Changeover time	30 minutes	1.5 hrs	
8.1.2a	Minor stoppages	complete study	not completed	
8.1.3a	Cracked castings	reduce 25%	reduced 5%	
8.1.3b	Warmup times	improve 15%	improved 10%	

Present Conditions

The implementation of TPM is on track. Initial successes in the pilot area are being replicated in other areas. But further work needs to be done. In particular, the number of reported safety violations is already 4 to date. This may be the result of better reporting, or because of increased maintenance involvement of operators who are insufficiently trained. The study on minor stoppages has not been completed, but is well under way. Progress on changeover time reduction is satisfactory, but not exceptional in areas other than the pilot area.

Outlook for Next Period

1) The deployment of TPM methods to all areas of the Production Department will be energized through a plantwide TPM "conference." Team Leader 1 will explain to his peers how increased involvement can improve work life, as well as improve equipment performance.

2) The study on minor stoppages will be completed during the next period. Once changeover gains have been stabilized in the pilot area, efforts will begin to identify and eliminate minor stoppages.

3) Safety awareness will be reinforced and each reported violation of regulations will be carefully analyzed to determine its root cause. Effective action will be taken to eliminate nonconforming conditions and practices.

graphs, Analysis Sheets, and Status Reports). In the traditional management structure, such information passes through very narrow channels and usually dead-ends before reaching a party who can do something meaningful with it. The deployment team's cross-functional review and analysis of frontline information ensures that information gets where it is needed for decision making.

Each month, the deployment team member (usually a department manager) who was assigned ownership of certain control points reviews the information received from each workcenter's reports about their checkpoints related to those control points. The department manager synthesizes this checkpoint information into combined and averaged results for the entire control point, expressing it in several places—on the Deployment Plan performance graph (monthly performance vs. targets), and on Analysis Sheets (Figure 7-7 shows one from the back of the Nonesuch Deployment Plan) and Status Reports (similar to the form in Figure 7-6, but summarizing for the deployment team/control point level).

In addition to serving as backup for the deployment team's cross-functional management of improvement activities, these documents are used to report information to the focus team, keeping them aware of progress in the control points that were critical to its annual policy theme.

FOCUS TEAM ADHERENCE ACTIVITIES

The role of the focus team during Adherence is to synthesize reported information to an even higher level. After activities have been carried on for some months, the focus team conducts a follow-up corporate diagnosis, looking for improvements in the critical keys for the current Strategic Improvement Cycle.

Complete the Plan Summary

All through the Strategic Improvement Cycle, the focus team tracks results for assignments outlined on the Confirmed Plan Summary—the document that resulted from playing catchball with the deployment teams during the Standardization phase. By the end of the improvement cycle, the plan summary should be filled in with actual results and completion dates for that cycle's activities (see Figure 7-8).

Deployment Plan Analysis Sheet

Nonesuch Casting Co.
Key: Lean equipment management
Control Point: Equipment/process improvement
Item #: 8.1
Item Owner: Engineering Manager   **Date Updated:**
Unit: Lean Equipment Management Initiative   **Next Review:**
          Review Team:

Implementation Issues

Issue	Owner	Resolution/Date
Small group activity not effective as evidenced by low number of implemented suggestions.	Production coordinator	Unresolved
Equipment cleanup not maintained, as evidenced by 5S audits by management.	Maintenance coordinator	Unresolved
TQM has little impact on operators, as evidenced by annual employee survey.	Engineering manager	Unresolved

ADHERENCE

FIGURE 7-7.
DEPLOYMENT PLAN ANALYSIS SHEET FOR
LEAN EQUIPMENT MANAGEMENT

Nonesuch Casting Co.

Plan Summary (Complete)

Date:

Critical Keys	Control Points/ Checkpoints	Item #	Owner	Strategy	Target	Actual	Start	Complete	Notes
Leadership		2	**President**	Lean Mgt. System	Done by:	complete	10/1/95	12/1/95	
	Business Renewal	2.1	"	Development Plan	12/1/95	complete	10/1/95	12/1/95	
	Focus	2.2	**Marketing manager**	Annual Policy	1/1/96	complete	12/1/95	1/1/96	
	Standardization	2.3	**President**	Action Plan	2/1/96	complete	1/1/96	2/1/96	
	Adherence	2.4a	**Production manager**	Self-Reports	3/1/96	complete	2/1/96	3/1/96	
		2.4b	"	Corporate Diagnosis	11/1/96	complete	10/1/96	11/1/96	
	Reflection	2.5	**President**	Analysis Summary	12/1/96	complete	11/1/96	12/1/96	
Lean equipment management		8	**Engineering manager**	Model equipment	OEE = 70%	OEE = 60%	3/1/96	11/1/96	
	Equip./process impr.	8.1	**Engineering manager**	Model equipment	OEE = 70%	OEE = 60%	3/1/96	12/1/96	
	Availability	8.1.1	Production coord./Maint. mgr.						
	Reduce breakdowns	8.1.1a	Production coord./Maint. mgr.	Model equipment	reduce 4%	reduced 3%	3/1/96	10/1/96	
	Reduce changeover time	8.1.1b	Production coord./Maint. mgr.	Model equipment	30 min.	45 min.	3/1/96	10/1/96	
	Performance efficiency	8.1.2	Engineering Manager						
	Reduce minor stoppages	8.1.2a	Eng. Manager/Toolroom coord.	Model equipment	study	complete	3/1/96	11/1/96	
	Quality	8.1.3	Eng. Manager/Production mgr.						
	Reduce cracking	8.1.3a	Eng. Manager/Production mgr.	Model equipment	reduce 25%	reduced 23%	1/1/96	12/1/96	
	Reduce warmups	8.1.3b	Eng. Manager/Production mgr.	Model equipment	reduce 15%	reduced 14%	1/1/96	11/1/96	
	Autonomous maint.	8.2	**Production Mgr./Maint. mgr.**	1st 3 steps of AM	pilot	complete	1/1/96	12/1/96	
	Initial cleaning	8.2.1	Maintenance manager	Step 1	major lines	complete	1/1/96	4/1/96	
	Sources of dirt	8.2.2	Maintenance technician	Step 2	pilot	80% done	5/1/96	10/1/96	
	Establish basic stds.	8.2.3	Maintenance manager	Step 3	pilot	complete	9/1/96	12/1/96	
	Safety	8.3	**Production manager**	DuPont program	LTA down 50%	complete	1/1/96	12/1/96	
	Initial audit	8.3.1	Production manager	DuPont program	by 2/1/96	complete	1/1/96	4/1/96	
	Establish standards	8.3.2	Production coordinator	On-Job-Training	all depts	complete	6/1/96	7/1/96	

FIGURE 7-8.
COMPLETED PLAN SUMMARY

Conduct a Corporate Diagnosis

Toward the end of the annual Strategic Improvement Cycle, the focus team should conduct another Corporate Diagnosis to assess the company-wide effects of policy implementation. The team records the new score on a Lean Management Scoreboard like the one in Figure 4-1 (see p. 51). For a strong visual display of the change, the team also adds new dots and lines on the Lean Radar Chart; use of a second color or symbol is helpful here to highlight changes. Figure 7-9 shows an updated Lean Radar Chart for Nonesuch Casting.

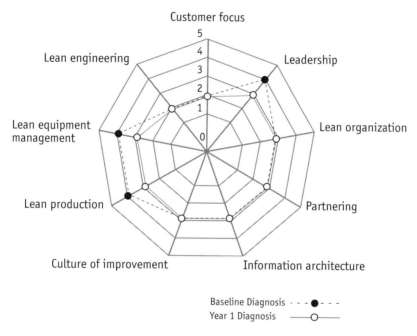

FIGURE 7-9.
UPDATED LEAN RADAR CHART

The purpose of this follow-up diagnosis is to understand how the company has progressed in each of the nine keys and to update the long-term Development Plan. By transferring the Corporate Diagnosis scores to the Development Plan, the focus team can spot areas of lagging progress that could require attention in the next year's annual policy. This information will be used in the final phase of the Strategic Improvement Cycle: Reflection.

THE STRATEGIC IMPROVEMENT CYCLE

		5 Levels of Organizational Learning				
Corner-stones of Growth	Keys to Development	Level 5	Level 4	Level 3	Level 2	Level 1
		Mass production	System initiation	System development	System maturity	System excellence
Strategy	1 Customer focus				Baseline, Year 1, Year 3	Year 5
	2 Leadership		Baseline	Year 1, Year 3	Year 5	
Structure	3 Lean organization			Baseline, Year 1, Year 3	Year 5	
	4 Partnering			Baseline, Year 1, Year 3	Year 5	
	5 Information architecture			Baseline, Year 1, Year 3	Year 5	
Strengths	6 Culture of improvement			Baseline, Year 1, Year 3	Year 5	
	7 Lean production		Baseline	Year 1, Year 3	Year 5	
	8 Lean equipment management		Baseline	Year 1	Year 3, Year 5	
	9 Lean engineering				Baseline, Year 1, Year 3	Year 5

FIGURE 7-10.
UPDATED DEVELOPMENT PLAN

On the Development Plan, the Nonesuch management team has previously recorded a baseline score determined from the initial Corporate Diagnosis during the Business Renewal Process. The plan also shows medium-term and long-term development targets and indicates strategic keys—the areas in which the company has committed itself to excellence over the long term. Following this first-year corporate diagnosis, the focus team adds new marks on the Development Plan to indicate how far the company has progressed in each key. The team notes especially any change in the critical keys targeted for improvement during the current Strategic Improvement Cycle. Figure 7-10 shows the results of the first annual follow-up diagnosis conducted by the Nonesuch Casting Company.

The Completed Plan Summary and Corporate Diagnosis results feed directly into the focus team's activities in Phase IV: Reflection.

NOTE

1. For more on the use of reporting in cross-functional management, see Yasuhiro Monden, *Toyota Management System: Linking the Seven Key Functional Areas* (Portland, Ore.: Productivity Press, 1993).

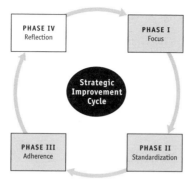

CHAPTER 8

Phase IV: Reflection

LIKE MODERN SOCIETY IN GENERAL, TRADITIONAL strategic planning rarely stops to reflect upon results, even if they are measured in a developmental framework such as the Nine Keys. In addition to an appropriate framework, proper reflection requires a Delta Zero mindset, a willingness to rethink the results desired as well as the factors required to achieve them. Throughout the previous phases of the strategic improvement cycle, the attitude of Delta Zero pervaded planning, policy deployment, and improvement activities in daily work. At the end of the cycle, the company's top leadership returns to Zero again, reviewing the overall results, problems, and surprises, and informing itself for building next year's policy.

In companies that have progressed one year or more beyond the Business Renewal Process, the focus team formally reviews the company's performance figures from the previous year to discover any gaps between actual performance and stated targets. The focus team also reviews assumptions made in its business renewal strategy—such as the importance of a product line to a particular customer—to see how they hold up against actual conditions and emerging trends. The outcome of this analysis is a list of assumption gaps and barriers to the company's continued progress towards its vision. Finally, the focus teams offers an evaluation of the prior year's policy, with suggestions for themes and keys to address in the coming strategic improvement cycle.

The Reflection phase entails the following steps:

1. Collect information
2. Identify critical performance gaps
3. Identify emergent gaps and barriers
4. Analyze gaps and barriers
5. Summarize

STEP 1. COLLECT INFORMATION

To reflect on policy implementation, the focus team collects information, developed during the previous Business Renewal Process or through regular business reporting during the year:

- the company vision and development plan
- financial reports for the previous year
- the company's Product/Market Matrix, Key Factor Matrix, and other strategic planning tools

The team also gathers documents generated during the Adherence phase:

- updated Lean Radar Chart and Development Plan
- the Completed Plan Summary for the prior year's activities
- a compilation of last year's Analysis Sheets and Status Reports from the deployment teams, as well as the focus team's notes from the latest Corporate Diagnosis

STEP 2. IDENTIFY CRITICAL PERFORMANCE GAPS

Next the focus team should identify the gaps between last year's improvement targets and the company's actual performance, as evidenced on the company's Plan Summary for the current improvement cycle. For example, Figure 7-8 (p. 134) showed Nonesuch Casting's Completed Plan

Summary. This chart indicates that Nonesuch reached its annual policy targets in the *leadership* key, and in some (but not all) of the control points for the *lean equipment management* key. In addition, the Lean Equipment Management Initiative deployment team's Analysis Sheet suggested the following gaps in anticipated performance:

- small group activity not effective, as evidenced by low number of implemented suggestions
- equipment cleanup not maintained, as evidenced by 5S audits by management
- TQM has little impact on operators, as evidenced by annual employee survey

If a company's list of performance gaps is long, the focus team should identify the most critical gaps to address. Ideally, there will be quantitative data to support analysis; in that case the team may use Pareto diagrams to rank gaps with the biggest impact on the business. Where only qualitative data are available, an affinity diagram may be used to group similar problems together for categorization. If necessary, voting methods may be used to narrow the field of problems to the most important.

STEP 3. IDENTIFY EMERGENT GAPS AND BARRIERS

In this step, the focus team questions the assumptions that support the company's business renewal strategy. The team begins by reviewing its market position using traditional strategic planning tools such as updated Product/Market Matrixes and Key Factor Matrixes (introduced in Chapter 4; see pp. 52–55).

After reviewing the strategic market information, the team brainstorms a list of emerging factors in the market that could keep the company from achieving top competitiveness. The team then uses the affinity diagram technique to group like factors together. If necessary, the team further subdivides these problems into smaller groups sharing common characteristics.

The data in the Nonesuch Casting affinity diagram shown in Figure 8-1 show that the Nonesuch management team believed that the company's

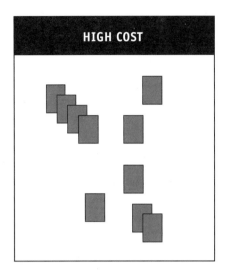

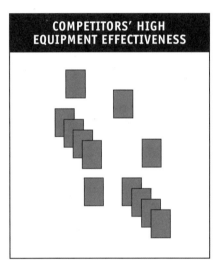

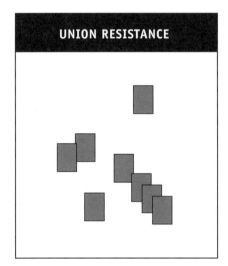

FIGURE 8-1.

AFFINITY DIAGRAM OF COMPETITIVE DISADVANTAGES

still-uncompetitive costs, new Asian rivals, the high equipment effectiveness of its established competitors, and union resistance to new manufacturing methods were the main competitive barriers facing the company.

STEP 4. ANALYZE GAPS AND BARRIERS

The next step of analysis uses a chart similar to the Target/Means Diagram introduced previously. First, the management team combines the lists of performance gaps and emergent barriers to its strategy, and analyzes the causes of each gap or barrier. The team sets up a cause-and-effect diagram for each gap or barrier, writing it on the effect side of the diagram. It then drafts a gap statement, suggests a target, and creates a performance graph showing industry, world class, and target levels. Next, the team gathers information about causes of each gap or barrier from sources such as departmental reviews, Analysis Sheets, or Status Reports, as well as additional factors suggested in a group brainstorm. Team members write the causal ideas or facts on Post-it Notes™ and place them on the cause-and-effect diagram. The team then uses the affinity diagram technique again to arrange these causes into groups. Header cards are created to summarize the major causes or causal types for each group. These become the labels for the fishbones.

The data in Figure 8-2 show that Nonesuch has identified uncompetitively high costs as one of its critical strategic gaps. Using Post-its, the management team entered on the chart all relevant information from the previous year's Review Sheets and Status Reports, as well as additional potential causes brainstormed by the group. Then, using the affinity diagram technique, they organized the Post-its into groups, above which they placed subject header cards. The header cards express the management team's understanding of the major causes of high cost.

STEP 5. SUMMARIZE

After the focus team has identified and analyzed critical performance and environmental gaps, it fills in an Analysis Summary. Keyed to the Completed Plan Summary, this document records the focus team's evaluation notes and recommendations for the focus of next year's annual policy (see Figure 8-3).

This evaluation lays the groundwork for the focus team to begin a new round of the Strategic Improvement Cycle. In many cases, the focus team can develop the theme for the new policy cycle directly from the recommendations in the Analysis Summary, without having to analyze and rank profit factors as it did in the first round (see Chapter 5). Top management will find that it is much more aware of the daily operation of the company than it was before the improvement cycle, and will understand better what it must do to continue its progress toward excellence in its strategic keys.

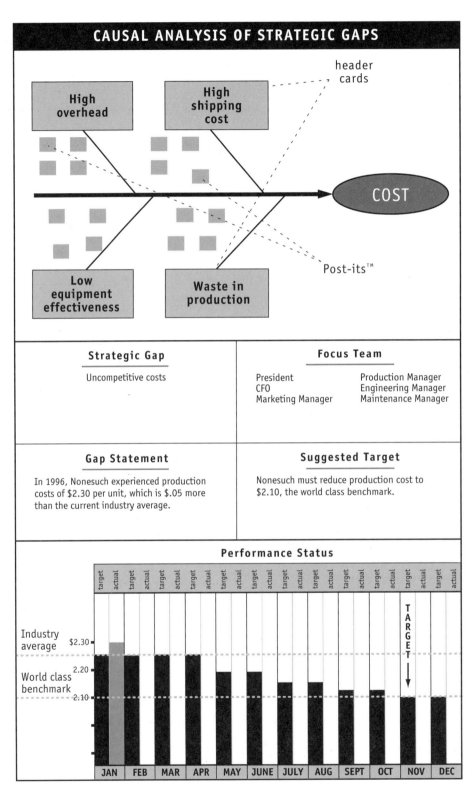

FIGURE 8-2.
ANALYSIS OF CAUSES OF A STRATEGIC GAP

Nonesuch Casting Co.　　　　**Analysis Summary**　　　　**Date:**

Critical Key	Control Points/ Checkpoints	#	Target	Actual	Evaluation	Recommendations
Leadership	**Business Renewal**	**1**	Done by:	complete	Top management team working well.	President of company should say what, when, and why, but not how.
	Focus	**2.1**	12/1/95	complete		
		2.2	1/1/96	complete		
	Standardization	**2.3**	2/1/96	complete	Although all activities were completed during Standardization, much resistance was encountered. There is still a legacy of mistrust between management and staff, and management and machine operators.	Stronger efforts to be made to combat low trust. Suggestion that next year's critical keys be Key 3, Lean organization, and Key 6, Culture of improvement.
	Finance	2.3.1	2/1/96	complete		
	Marketing	2.3.2	2/1/96	complete		
	Production	2.3.3	2/1/96	complete		
	Engineering	2.3.4	2/1/96	complete		
	Maintenance	2.3.5	2/1/96	complete		
	Lean Equip. Mgt. Init.	2.3.6	2/1/96	complete		
	Adherence	**2.4**	3/1/96	complete	Adherence activities are pro forma because of low trust. Workers still see reporting activity as a job that they aren't being paid to do. Results in Lean Equipment Management pilot area are promising, however.	
	Finance	2.4.1	3/1/96	complete		
	Marketing	2.4.2	3/1/96	complete		
	Production	2.4.3	3/1/96	complete		
	Engineering	2.4.4	3/1/96	complete		
	Maintenance	2.4.5	3/1/96	complete		
	Lean Equip. Mgt. Init.	2.4.6	3/1/96	complete		
	Focus Team (Corp. Diag.)	2.4.7	11/1/96	complete		
	Reflection	**2.5**	12/15/96	complete	Enthusiastic participation.	Reclassify as part of normal control activity.
Lean equipment management		**8**	OEE = 70%	OEE = 60%		
	Equip./process impr.	**8.1**	OEE = 70%	OEE = 60%	Equipment/process improvement program is still active after one year. But performance is generally less than expected in most areas.	
	Reduce breakdowns	8.1.1a	reduce 4%	reduce 3%		
	Reduce changeover time	8.1.1b	30 min.	45 min.		
	Reduce minor stoppages	8.1.2	study	complete		
	Reduce cracking	8.1.3a	reduce 25%	reduce 23%		
	Reduce warmups	8.1.3b	reduce 15%	reduce 14%		
	Autonomous maint.	**8.2**	pilot	complete	Steps 1–3 completed on pilot line. Work proceeds on containing sources of dirt and contamination on pilot line.	Implement Steps 2–3 on major lines where cleaning has been completed. Begin to spread AM to other areas
	Initial cleaning	8.2.1	major lines	complete		
	Sources of dirt	8.2.2	pilot	80% done		
	Establish basic stds.	8.2.3	pilot	complete		
	Safety	**8.3**	LTA down 50%	complete	Safety problems originally underestimated.	
	Initial audit	8.3.1	by 2/1/96	complete		
	Establish standards	8.3.2	all depts	complete		

FIGURE 8-3.
ANALYSIS SUMMARY

Continuing the Cycle of Organizational Learning

ORGANIZATIONS THAT SUCCEED AT LEAN PRODUCTION have three things in common:

- a carefully designed and maintained web of cooperative human relations
- a system for continuously upgrading the technical and problem-solving skills of all employees
- relentless systematic study and application throughout the organization to improve quality, speed, cost, and flexibility in production and in all business processes

The Lean Management System promotes lean production by providing a framework for integrating these three factors and strengthening them in the direction appropriate to the long-term growth of the company. Together these factors express the spirit of Delta Zero, an approach that constantly redefines what it means to be "best in the world."

The essence of the Lean Management System is an expanded flow of information within the company and a continuously enhanced ability to learn from that information how to improve the process. As the preceding chapters have shown, the Lean Management System is based on cycles of organizational learning in all areas of the company. Its premise is that the most valuable asset in a lean and profitable manufacturing company isn't the expensive equipment, but the technology of its production and information processes—most of which resides in the people of the company, not in the machines.

It is not machines that produce things. Productivity is an effect of human beings working together. Machines are merely an extension of their collective imagination and energy. Lean management is based on a cultural system of organizational growth and a deep understanding of how people work together. In particular, it is a system designed for successfully managing and developing teams of educated, motivated, and responsible people. It is a culture because it defines a style, an open, cooperative approach to communication, deliberation, and action. It is a culture because it defines what human action is about: quantum leaps of improvement—in a word, *growth*.

Ultimately it is easier to replace a machine than it is to regain a lost customer, or to rebuild the complex network of relationships between managers, employees, suppliers, and distributors. It is difficult to master the complicated routines that coordinate management, employees, suppliers, and distributors in producing and delivering what the customer has ordered—and on time. It is impossible to replace a company's unique spirit: its vitality and ability to recognize opportunity, to create new products, to learn new procedures, and to forge relations with new customers in new markets. That is why world class companies in Japan and elsewhere invest heavily in the development of their human resources—and generally outperform competitors that focus on new equipment while neglecting the process knowledge and improvement ability of their employees.

The Lean Management System works. It raises quality, productivity, flexibility, and employee morale, and it requires relatively little capital investment. At the heart of the lean management culture is a profound new attitude toward universal human intelligence and creativity, which we have tried to capture in the concept of Delta Zero. To succeed in the lean production revolution, you must put your people first and champion the new culture. You must reorganize to work as a set of linked teams. You must involve all your employees. In particular you must lead your management team into the new era by demonstrating the new culture in everything you do. This requires a fresh approach to the meaning of work, technology, even your own career. It requires releasing the constraints of old paradigms. It is a wise sacrifice for the continued growth and development of your organization in the decades ahead.

For Further Reading

LEAN PRODUCTION

Swartz, James B. *The Hunters and the Hunted: A Non-Linear Solution for Reengineering the Workplace.* Portland, Ore.: Productivity Press, 1994.

Womack, James P., Daniel T. Jones, and Daniel Roos. *The Machine That Changed the World.* New York: Rawson Associates, 1990.

TOYOTA PRODUCTION SYSTEM AND JUST-IN-TIME

Hirano, Hiroyuki. *JIT Factory Revolution: A Pictorial Guide to Factory Design of the Future.* Portland, Ore.: Productivity Press, 1989.

Hirano, Hiroyuki. *JIT Implementation Manual: The Complete Guide to Just-in-Time Manufacturing.* Portland, Ore: Productivity Press, 1990.

Japan Management Association, ed. *Kanban and Just-in-Time at Toyota: Management Begins at the Workplace* (revised ed.). Portland, Ore.: Productivity Press, 1989.

Ohno, Taiichi. *Toyota Production System: Beyond Large-Scale Production.* Portland, Ore.: Productivity Press, 1988.

Shingo, Shigeo. *A Study of the Toyota Production System from an Industrial Engineering Viewpoint.* Portland, Ore.: Productivity Press, 1989.

STRATEGIC PLANNING

Christopher, William F. *Vision, Mission, Total Quality: Leadership Tools for Turbulent Times.* Portland, Ore.: Productivity Press, 1994.

Miltenburg, John. *Manufacturing Strategy: How to Formulate and Implement a Winning Plan.* Portland, Ore.: Productivity Press, 1995.

Mintzberg, Henry. *The Rise and Fall of Strategic Planning.* New York: Prentice-Hall, 1994.

Moore, J.I. *Writers on Strategy and Strategic Management.* London: Penguin, 1992.

Ohmae, Kenichi. *The Mind of the Strategist.* New York: McGraw-Hill, 1982.

AFFINITY DIAGRAMS/7 NEW MANAGEMENT TOOLS

Asaka, Tesuichi, and Kazuo Ozeki, eds. *Handbook of Quality Tools: The Japanese Approach.* Portland, Ore.: Productivity Press, 1990.

Mizuno, Shigeru, ed. *Management for Quality Improvement: The 7 New QC Tools.* Portland, Ore.: Productivity Press, 1988.

CORPORATE DIAGNOSIS

Jackson, Thomas L., with Constance E. Dyer. *Corporate Diagnosis: Meeting Global Standards of Excellence.* Portland, Ore.: Productivity Press, 1996.

Kobayashi, Iwao. *20 Keys to Workplace Improvement* (revised ed.). Portland, Ore.: Productivity Press, 1995.

POLICY DEPLOYMENT (HOSHIN MANAGEMENT)

Akao, Yoji. *Hoshin Kanri: Policy Deployment for Successful TQM.* Portland, Ore.: Productivity Press, 1991.

CROSS-FUNCTIONAL MANAGEMENT

Dimancescu, Dan. *The Seamless Enterprise: Making Cross Functional Management Work.* New York: Harper Business, 1992.

Ishikawa, Kaoru. *What Is Total Quality Control?* Englewood Cliffs, NJ: Prentice-Hall, 1985.

Meyer, Christopher. *Fast Cycle Time.* New York: Free Press, 1993.

Monden, Yasuhiro. *Toyota Management System: Linking the Seven Key Functional Areas.* Portland, Ore.: Productivity Press, 1993.

Rummler, Geary A. and Alan P. Brache. *Improving Performance: How to Manage the White Space on the Organizational Chart.* San Francisco: Jossey-Bass, 1990.

PERFORMANCE MEASUREMENT

Kaydos, Will. *Measuring, Managing, and Maximizing Performance.* Portland, Ore.: Productivity Press, 1991.

Maskell, Brian. *Performance Measurement for World Class Manufacturing: A Model for American Companies.* Portland, Ore.: Productivity Press, 1991.

ORGANIZATIONAL LEARNING

Morecroft, John D. W., and John D. Sterman, eds. *Modeling for Learning Organizations.* Portland, Ore.: Productivity Press, 1994.

Chawla, Sarita, and John Renesch, eds. *Learning Organizations.* Portland, Ore.: Productivity Press, 1995.

QUICK CHANGEOVER

Sekine, Kenichi, and Keisuke Arai. *Kaizen for Quick Changeover: Going Beyond SMED.* Portland, Ore.: Productivity Press, 1992.

Shingo, Shigeo. *Quick Changeover for Operators.* Portland, Ore.: Productivity Press, 1996.

Shingo, Shigeo. *A Revolution in Manufacturing: The SMED System.* Portland, Ore.: Productivity Press, 1985.

MISTAKE-PROOFING (POKA-YOKE)

Nikkan Kogyo Shimbun, Ltd. and *Factory Magazine,* eds. *Poka-Yoke: Improving Product Quality by Preventing Defects.* Portland, Ore.: Productivity Press, 1989.

Shingo, Shigeo. *Zero Quality Control: Source Inspection and the Poka-yoke System.* Portland, Ore.: Productivity Press, 1986.

CEDAC

Fukuda, Ryuji. *CEDAC: A Tool for Continuous Systematic Improvement.* Portland, Ore.: Productivity Press, 1990.

Fukuda, Ryuji. *Managerial Engineering: Techniques for Improving Quality and Productivity in the Workplace.* Portland, Ore.: Productivity Press, 1986.

5S AND VISUAL CONTROLS

Greif, Michel. *The Visual Factory: Building Participation Through Shared Information.* Portland, Ore.: Productivity Press, 1991.

Hirano, Hiroyuki. *5 Pillars of the Visual Workplace: The Sourcebook for 5S Implementation.* Portland, Ore.: Productivity Press, 1995.

Hirano, Hiroyuki. *5S for Operators.* Portland, Ore.: Productivity Press, 1996.

Nikkan Kogyo Shimbun, ed. *Visual Control Systems.* Portland, Ore.: Productivity Press, 1995.

TPM

Japan Institute of Plant Maintenance, ed. *TPM for Every Operator.* Portland, Ore.: Productivity Press, 1996.

Nakajima, Seiichi, ed. *TPM Development Program: Implementing Total Productive Maintenance.* Portland, Ore.: Productivity Press, 1989.

Robinson, Charles J., and Andrew P. Ginder. *Implementing TPM: The North American Experience.* Portland, Ore.: Productivity Press, 1995.

Shirose, Kunio, ed. *TPM Team Guide.* Portland, Ore.: Productivity Press, 1995.

Suzuki, Tokutaro, ed. *TPM in Process Industries.* Portland, Ore.: Productivity Press, 1994.

TQM

Barrett, Derm. *Fast Focus on TQM: A Concise Guide to Companywide Learning.* Portland, Ore.: Productivity Press, 1994.

Galgano, Alberto. *Companywide Quality Management.* Portland, Ore.: Productivity Press, 1994.

Périgord, Michel. *Achieving Total Quality Management: A Program for Action.* Portland, Ore.: Productivity Press, 1991.

Shiba, Shoji, Alan Graham, and David Walden. *A New American TQM: Four Practical Revolutions in Management.* Portland, Ore.: Productivity Press, 1993.

STANDARDIZATION

Nakamura, Shigehiro. *The New Standardization: Keystone of Continuous Improvement in Manufacturing.* Portland, Ore.: Productivity Press, 1993.

About the Authors

THOMAS L. JACKSON

DR. JACKSON FIRST BECAME INTERESTED in business and economics while working as a lawyer at the Department of Energy, where he managed requests for exceptions to price regulations on gasoline during the Oil Crises of 1978. After leaving government in 1980, he studied economics and international business at Indiana University School of Business, and graduated with an M.B.A. and a Ph.D. in business economics.

In 1989, Dr. Jackson was asked to become a consulting editor for Productivity Press. Through his association with Productivity, he first became aware of the Toyota production system and the revolution it is causing throughout the business world. In 1991, Productivity CEO Norman Bodek invited him to become a manufacturing consultant overseas, and in 1992, Dr. Jackson became managing director of SEA Productivity Sdn. Bhd., a joint venture with Productivity, Inc. in southeast Asia. In 1995, he returned to the United States to become vice president of product development for Productivity, Inc. Dr. Jackson's clients include BHP Steel, Ford Motor Company, National Semiconductor, Nestle, Nissan, Otis Elevator, Pharmmalaysia, Perelli Cables (Australia), QDOS Microcircuits, and Xerox Mexicana. He lives with his wife, Daksha, in Portland, Oregon.

KAREN R. JONES

MS. JONES IS SENIOR DEVELOPMENT EDITOR with Productivity Press, where she has also served as a series acquisition editor and as managing editor. Since joining Productivity Press in 1987, she has overseen the development of many leading-edge works on manufacturing process improvement, quality management, and workplace creativity, including *Caught in the Middle, The Benchmarking Workbook,* and *20 Keys to Workplace Improvement.* She is a regular reviewer for two Productivity monthly newsletters, *Total Employee Involvement* and *Total Productive Maintenance.*

Ms. Jones holds fine arts and law degrees from Indiana University and a master's in library science from the University of Michigan. Before coming to Productivity she served as an associate attorney with Esdaile, Barrett & Esdaile in Boston, Massachusetts, and as a manuscript editor with the law book division of Little, Brown & Co. in Boston. She lives in Portland, Oregon.

Index

BOOKS FROM PRODUCTIVITY, INC.

Productivity, Inc. publishes books that empower individuals and companies to achieve excellence in quality, productivity, and the creative involvement of all employees. Through steadfast efforts to support the vision and strategy of continuous improvement, Productivity, Inc. delivers today's leading-edge tools and techniques gathered directly from industrial leaders around the world.

Call toll-free 1-800-394-6868 for our free catalog.

---

20 KEYS TO WORKPLACE IMPROVEMENT
Iwao Kobayashi

The 20 Keys system does more than just bring together twenty of the world's top manufacturing improvement approaches—it integrates these individual methods into a closely interrelated system for revolutionizing every aspect of your manufacturing organization. This revised edition of Kobayashi's best-seller amplifies the synergistic power of raising the levels of all these critical areas simultaneously. The new edition presents upgraded criteria for the five-level scoring system in most of the 20 Keys, supporting your progress toward becoming not only best in your industry but best in the world. New material and an updated layout throughout assist managers in implementing this comprehensive approach. In addition, valuable case studies describe how Morioka Seiko (Japan) advanced in Key 18 (use of microprocessors) and how Windfall Products (Pennsylvania) adapted the 20 Keys to its situation with good results.
ISBN 1-56327-109-5 / 304 pages / $50.00 / Order 20KREV-B256

BECOMING LEAN
Inside Stories of U.S. Manufacturers
Jeffrey Liker

Most other books on lean management focus on technical methods and offer a picture of what a lean system should look like. Some provide snapshots of before and after. This is the first book to provide technical descriptions of successful solutions and performance improvements. The first book to include powerful first-hand accounts of the complete process of change, its impact on the entire organization, and the rewards and benefits of becoming lean. At the heart of this book you will find the stories of American manufacturers who have successfully implemented lean methods. Authors offer personalized accounts of their organization's lean transformation, including struggles and successes, frustrations and surprises. Now you have a unique opportunity to go inside their implementation process to see what worked, what didn't, and why. Many of these executives and managers who led the charge to becoming lean in their organizations tell their stories here for the first time!
ISBN 1-56327-173-7 / 350 pages / $35.00 / Order LEAN-B256

Productivity, Inc. Dept. BK, P.O. Box 13390, Portland, OR 97213-0390
Telephone: 1-800-394-6868   Fax: 1-800-394-6286

CORPORATE DIAGNOSIS
Meeting Global Standards for Excellence
Thomas L. Jackson with Constance E. Dyer

All too often, strategic planning neglects an essential first step—and final step—diagnosis of the organization's current state. What's required is a systematic review of the critical factors in organizational learning and growth, factors that require monitoring, measurement, and management to ensure that your company competes successfully. This executive workbook provides a step-by-step method for diagnosing an organization's strategic health and measuring its overall competitiveness against world class standards. With checklists, charts, and detailed explanations, *Corporate Diagnosis* is a practical instruction manual. The pillars of Jackson's diagnostic system are strategy, structure, and capability. Detailed diagnostic questions in each area are provided as guidelines for developing your own self-assessment survey.
ISBN 1-56327-086-2 / 115 pages / $65.00 / Order CDIAG-B256

CYCLE TIME MANAGEMENT
The Fast Track to Time-Based Productivity Improvement
Patrick Northey and Nigel Southway

As much as 90 percent of the operational activities in a traditional plant are nonessential or pure waste. This book presents a proven methodology for eliminating this waste within 24 to 30 months by measuring productivity in terms of time instead of revenue or people. CTM is a cohesive management strategy that integrates just-in-time (JIT) production, computer integrated manufacturing (CIM), and total quality control (TQC). From this succinct, highly focused book, you'll learn what CTM is, how to implement it, and how to manage it.
ISBN 1-56327-015-3 / 200 pages / $30.00 / Order CYCLE-B256

THE HUNTERS AND THE HUNTED
A Non-Linear Solution for Reengineering the Workplace
James B. Swartz

Our competitive environment changes rapidly. If you want to survive, you have to stay on top of those changes. Otherwise, you become prey to your competitors. Hunters continuously change and learn; anyone who doesn't becomes the hunted and sooner or later will be devoured. This unusual non-fiction novel provides a veritable crash course in continuous transformation. It offers lessons from real-life companies and introduces many industrial gurus as characters. *The Hunters and the Hunted* doesn't simply tell you how to change; it puts you inside the change process itself.
ISBN 1-56327-043-9 / 582 pages / $45.00 / Order HUNT-B256

Productivity, Inc. Dept. BK, P.O. Box 13390, Portland, OR 97213-0390
Telephone: 1-800-394-6868   Fax: 1-800-394-6286

INTRODUCTION TO TPM
Total Productive Maintenance
Seiichi Nakajima

Total Productive Maintenance (TPM) combines preventive maintenance with Japanese concepts of total quality control (TQC) and total employee involvement (TEI). The result is a new system for equipment maintenance that optimizes effectiveness, eliminates breakdowns, and promotes autonomous operator maintenance through day-to-day activities. Since it was first introduced in Japan, TPM has caused a worldwide revolution in plant maintenance. Here are the steps involved in TPM and case examples from top Japanese plants.
ISBN 0-915299-23-2 / 149 pages / $45.00 / Order ITPM-B256

JIT FACTORY REVOLUTION
A Pictorial Guide to Factory Design of the Future
Hiroyuki Hirano

The first encyclopedic picture-book of Just-In-Time, using photos and diagrams to show exactly how JIT looks and functions in production and assembly plants. Unprecedented behind-the-scenes look at multiprocess handling, cell technology, quick changeovers, kanban, andon, and other visual control systems. See why a picture is worth a thousand words.
ISBN 0-915299-44-5 / 218 pages / $50.00 / Order JITFAC-B256

KAIZEN FOR QUICK CHANGEOVER
Going Beyond SMED
Kenichi Sekine and Keisuke Arai

Especially useful for manufacturing managers and engineers, this book describes exactly how to achieve faster changeover. Picking up where Shingo's SMED book left off, you'll learn how to streamline the process even further to reduce changeover time and optimize staffing at the same time.
ISBN 0-915299-38-0 / 315 pages / $75.00 / Order KAIZEN-B256

KANBAN AND JUST-IN-TIME AT TOYOTA
Management Begins at the Workplace
Japan Management Association
Translated by David J. Lu

Toyota's world-renowned success proves that with kanban, the Just-In-Time production system (JIT) makes most other manufacturing practices obsolete. This simple but powerful classic is based on seminars given by JIT creator Taiichi Ohno to introduce Toyota's own supplier companies to JIT. It shows how to implement the world's most efficient production system. A clear and complete introduction.
ISBN 0-915299-48-8 / 211 pages / $40.00 / Order KAN-B256

Productivity, Inc. Dept. BK, P.O. Box 13390, Portland, OR 97213-0390
Telephone: 1-800-394-6868   Fax: 1-800-394-6286

MANUFACTURING STRATEGY
How to Formulate and Implement a Winning Plan
John Miltenburg

This book offers a step-by-step method for creating a strategic manufacturing plan. The key tool is a multidimensional worksheet that links the competitive analysis to manufacturing outputs, the seven basic production systems, the levels of capability and the levers for moving to a higher level. The author presents each element of the worksheet and shows you how to link them to create an integrated strategy and implementation plan. By identifying the appropriate production system for your business, you can determine what output you can expect from manufacturing, how to improve outputs, and how to change to more optimal production systems as your business needs change.
ISBN 1-56327-071-4 / 391 pages / $45.00 / Order MANST-B256

POKA-YOKE
Improving Product Quality by Preventing Defects
Nikkan Kogyo Shimbun Ltd. and Factory Magazine (ed.)

If your goal is 100 percent zero defects, here is the book for you—a completely illustrated guide to poka-yoke (mistake-proofing) for supervisors and shop-floor workers. Many poka-yoke devices come from line workers and are implemented with the help of engineering staff. The result is better product quality—and greater participation by workers in efforts to improve your processes, your products, and your company as a whole.
ISBN 0-915299-31-3 / 295 pages / $65.00 / Order IPOKA-B256

QUICK RESPONSE MANUFACTURING
A Companywide Approach to Reducing Lead Times
Rajan Suri

Quick Response Manufacturing (QRM) is an expansion of time-based competition (TBC) strategies, which use speed for a competitive advantage. Essentially, QRM stems from a single principle: to reduce lead times. But unlike other time-based competition strategies, QRM is an approach for the entire organization, from the front desk to the shop floor, from purchasing to sales. In order to truly succeed with speed-based competition, you must adopt the approach *throughout* the organization.
ISBN 1-56327-201-6/ 560 pages / $50.00 / Order QRM-B256

A REVOLUTION IN MANUFACTURING
The SMED System
Shigeo Shingo

The heart of JIT is quick changeover methods. Dr. Shingo, inventor of the Single-Minute Exchange of Die (SMED) system for Toyota, shows you how to reduce your changeovers by an average of 98 percent! By applying Shingo's techniques, you'll see rapid improvements (lead time reduced from weeks to days, lower inventory and warehousing costs) that will improve quality, productivity, and profits.
ISBN 0-915299-03-8 / 383 pages / $75.00 / Order SMED-B256

Productivity, Inc. Dept. BK, P.O. Box 13390, Portland, OR 97213-0390
Telephone: 1-800-394-6868   Fax: 1-800-394-6286

TOOL NAVIGATOR
A Master Guide for Teams
Walter J. Michalski

Are you constantly searching for just the right tool to help your team efforts? Do you find yourself not sure which to use next? Here's the largest tool compendium of facilitation and problem solving tools you'll find. Each tool is presented in a two to three page spread which describes the tool, its use, how to implement it, and an example. Charts provide a matrix to help you choose the right tool for your needs. Plus, you can combine tools to help your team navigate through any problem solving or improvement process. Use these tools for all seasons: team building, idea generating, data collecting, analyzing/trending, evaluating/selecting, decision making, planning/presenting, and more!
ISBN 1-56327-178-8 / 550 pages / $150.00 / Order NAVI1-B256

TOYOTA PRODUCTION SYSTEM
Beyond Large-Scale Production
Taiichi Ohno

Here's the first information ever published in Japan on the Toyota production system (known as Just-In-Time manufacturing). Here Ohno, who created JIT for Toyota, reveals the origins, daring innovations, and ceaseless evolution of the Toyota system into a full management system. You'll learn how to manage JIT from the man who invented it, and to create a winning JIT environment in your own manufacturing operation.
ISBN 0-915299-14-3 / 163 pages / $45.00 / Order OTPS-B256

TPM FOR AMERICA
What It Is and Why You Need It
Herbert R. Steinbacher and Norma L. Steinbacher

As much as 15 to 40 percent of manufacturing costs are attributable to maintenance. With a fully implemented TPM program, your company can eradicate all but a fraction of these costs. Co-written by an American TPM practitioner and an experienced educator, this book gives a convincing account of why American companies must adopt TPM if they are to successfully compete in world markets. Includes examples from leading American companies showing how TPM has changed them into more efficient and productive organizations.
ISBN 1-56327-044-7 / 169 pages / $25.00 / Order TPMAM-256

TPM IN PROCESS INDUSTRIES
Tokutaro Suzuki (ed.)

Process industries have a particularly urgent need for collaborative equipment management systems like TPM that can absolutely guarantee safe, stable operation. In TPM in Process Industries, top consultants from JIPM (Japan Institute of Plant Maintenance) document approaches to implementing TPM in process industries. They focus on the process environment and equipment issues such as process loss structure and calculation, autonomous maintenance, equipment and process improvement, and quality maintenance. Must reading for any manager in the process industry.
ISBN 1-56327-036-6 / 400 pages / $85.00 / Order TPMPI-B256

Productivity, Inc. Dept. BK, P.O. Box 13390, Portland, OR 97213-0390
Telephone: 1-800-394-6868   Fax: 1-800-394-6286

VISUAL CONTROL SYSTEMS

Nikkan Kogyo Shimbun (ed.)

Every day, progressive companies all over the world are making manufacturing improvements that profoundly impact productivity, quality, and lead time. Case studies of the most innovative visual control systems in Japanese companies have been gathered, translated, and compiled in this notebook. No other source provides more insightful information on recent developments in Japanese manufacturing technology. Plant managers, VPs of operations, and CEOs with little spare time need a concise and timely means of staying informed. Here's a gold mine of ideas for reducing costs and delivery times and improving quality.
ISBN 1-56327-143-5 / 189 pages / $30.00 / Order VCSP-B256

ZERO QUALITY CONTROL

Source Inspection and the Poka-Yoke System

Shigeo Shingo

Dr. Shingo reveals his unique defect prevention system, which combines source inspection and poka-yoke (mistake-proofing) devices that provide instant feedback on errors before they can become defects. The result: 100 percent inspection that eliminates the need for SQC and produces defect-free products without fail. Includes 112 examples, most costing under $100. Two-part video program also available; call for details.
ISBN 0-915299-07-0 / 328 pages / $75.00 / Order ZQC-B256

TO ORDER: Write, phone, or fax Productivity, Inc., Dept. BK, P.O. Box 13390, Portland, OR 97213-0390, phone 1-800-394-6868, fax 1-800-394-6286. Send check or charge to your credit card (American Express, Visa, MasterCard accepted).

U.S. ORDERS: Add $5 shipping for first book, $2 each additional for UPS surface delivery. Add $5 for each AV program containing 1 or 2 tapes; add $12 for each AV program containing 3 or more tapes. We offer attractive quantity discounts for bulk purchases of individual titles; call for more information.

ORDER BY E-MAIL: Order 24 hours a day from anywhere in the world. Use either address:

      To order: **service@productivityinc.com**
      To view the online catalog and/or order: **http://www.productivityinc.com/**

QUANTITY DISCOUNTS: For information on quantity discounts, please contact our sales department.

INTERNATIONAL ORDERS: Write, phone, or fax for quote and indicate shipping method desired. For international callers, telephone number is 503-235-0600 and fax number is 503-235-0909. Prepayment in U.S. dollars must accompany your order (checks must be drawn on U.S. banks). When quote is returned with payment, your order will be shipped promptly by the method requested.

NOTE: Prices are in U.S. dollars and are subject to change without notice.

About the Shopfloor Series

Put powerful and proven improvement tools in the hands of your entire workforce!

Progressive shopfloor improvement techniques are imperative for manufacturers who want to stay competitive and to achieve world class excellence. And it's the comprehensive education of all shopfloor workers that ensures full participation and success when implementing new programs. The Shopfloor Series books make practical information accessible to everyone by presenting major concepts and tools in simple, clear language and at a reading level that has been adjusted for operators by skilled instructional designers. One main idea is presented every two to four pages so that the book can be picked up and put down easily. Each chapter begins with an overview and ends with a summary section. Helpful illustrations are used throughout.

Other books currently in the Shopfloor Series:

5S FOR OPERATORS
5 Pillars of the Visual Workplace
The Productivity Development Team
ISBN 1-56327-123-0 / 133 pages
Order 5SOP-B256 / $25.00

QUICK CHANGEOVER FOR OPERATORS
The SMED System
The Productivity Development Team
ISBN 1-56327-125-7 / 93 pages
Order QCOOP-B256 / $25.00

MISTAKE-PROOFING FOR OPERATORS
The Productivity Development Team
ISBN 1-56327-127-3 / 93 pages
Order ZQCOP-B256 / $25.00

JUST-IN-TIME FOR OPERATORS
The Productivity Development Team
ISBN 1-56327-133-8 / 84 pages
Order JITOP-B256 / $25.00

TPM FOR SUPERVISORS
The Productivity Development Team
ISBN 1-56327-161-3 / 96 pages
Order TPMSUP-B256 / $25.00

TPM TEAM GUIDE
Kunio Shirose
ISBN 1-56327-079-X / 175 pages
Order TGUIDE-B256 / $25.00

AUTONOMOUS MAINTENANCE
Japan Institute of Plant Maintenance
ISBN 1-56327-082-X / 138 pages
Order AUTMOP-B256 / $25.00

FOCUSED EQUIPMENT IMPROVEMENT
FOR TPM TEAMS
Japan Institute of Plant Maintenance
ISBN 1-56327-081-1 / 138 pages
Order FEIOP-B256 / $25.00

TPM FOR EVERY OPERATOR
Japan Institute of Plant Maintenance
ISBN 1-56327-080-3 / 136 pages
Order TPMEO-B256 / $25.00

OEE FOR OPERATORS
Overall Equipment Effectiveness
The Productivity Development Team
ISBN 1-56327-221-0 / 96 pages
Order OEEOP-B256 / $25.00

CELLULAR MANUFACTURING
The Productivity Development Team
ISBN 1-56327-213-X / 96 pages
Order CELLP-B256 / $25.00

Productivity, Inc. Dept. BK, P.O. Box 13390, Portland, OR 97213-0390
Telephone: 1-800-394-6868   Fax: 1-800-394-6286

Productivity, Inc. Consulting and Public Events

Productivity, Inc. is the leading American consulting, training, and publishing company focusing on delivering improvement technology to the global manufacturing industry.

Productivity, Inc. prides itself on delivering today's leading performance improvement tools and methodologies to enhance rapid, ongoing, measurable results. Whether you need assistance with long-term planning or focused, results-driven training, Productivity, Inc.'s world-class consultants can enhance your pursuit of competitive advantage. In concert with your management team, Productivity, Inc. will focus on implementing the principles of Value-Adding Management, Total Quality Management, Just-in-Time, and Total Productive Maintenance. Each approach is supported by Productivity's wide array of team-based tools: Standardization, One-Piece Flow, Hoshin Planning, Quick Changeover, Mistake-Proofing, Kanban, Problem Solving with CEDAC, Visual Workplace, Visual Office, Autonomous Maintenance, Overall Equipment Effectiveness, Design of Experiments, Quality Function Deployment, Ergonomics, and more! And, based on continuing research, Productivity, Inc. expands its offering every year.

Productivity, Inc.'s conferences provide an excellent opportunity to interact with the best of the best. Each year our national conferences bring together the leading practitioners of world-class, high-performance strategies. Our workshops, forums, plant tours, and master series are scheduled throughout the U.S. to provide the opportunity for continuous improvement in key areas of lean management and production.

Productivity, Inc. is known for significant improvement on the shop floor and the bottom line. Through years of repeat business, an expanding and loyal client base continues to recommend Productivity, Inc. to their colleagues. Contact Productivity, Inc. to learn how we can tailor our services to fit your needs.

Product-Market Matrix

Workcenter Control Board

vision

CORPORATE DIAGNOSIS

Delta Zero

system development

structure

Analysis Summary

control points

lean engineering

Lean Management S

action team

loyment Plan

lean production

Team Action Plan

customer focus

mass producti

strategy

Daily Planner

Key Factor Matrix

lean organization

Monthly Self-Reports

three cornerstones of growth

trengths

Development Plan

Monthly Planner

LEAN RADAR CHART

WORKCENTER CONTROL

Strategic

Business Renewal Process

FOCUS

contr

checkpoints

five levels o